Leadership Perception of Problems and Prospects of Panchayats in Bihar with Special Reference to Panchayats in Naugachia Sub-Division of Bhagalpur District

Dr. Murlidhar Mandal

BONFRING™
Intellectual Integrity

Leadership Perception of Problems and Prospects Of Panchayats in Bihar with Special Reference to Panchayats In Naugachia Sub-Division of Bhagalpur District

9 789383 459254 >

ISBN 978-93-83459-25-4

Author

Dr. Murlidhar Mandal
Guest Lecturer (political Science)
J.M.S. College, Munger, Tilka Manjhi Bhagalpur University,
Bhagalpur, India.

Published by

Bonfring
292/2, 5th Street Extension, Gandhipuram,
Coimbatore-641 012.
Tamilnadu, India.
E-mail: info@bonfring.org
Website: www.bonfring.org
Contact: 0422 3928700

ABOUT AUTHOR

Dr. Murlidhar Mandal (b. 1976) obtained his M.A.,B.LibJournalism and Ph.D. degrees in Political Science from the T.M.B. University Bhagalpur. He has been teaching Political Science at the undergraduate level at JMS College Munger TMB University Bhagalpur since September 2013 and has taught at the undergraduate level at Bihar Sharaph Nalanda Since 2009 .

His areas of specialization include International Law, International Organization.He has also worked on Social Health in (ORG)Operation Research Group Marketing. He has presented a number of papers on   political science ,democracy of India ,Banking, Human Right ,Women Empowerment and environmental issues at various National and International Seminars, Journal and Conferences.

He is an active member of the All Indian Political Science Association, Bihar Political Science Association ,Indian Institute of Public Administration, Jabalpur Management Association and is associated with a number of academic organizations. Dr. Mandal has been a member of the Gandhi Bihar Manch Bhagalpur Bihar .

Apart from these he has also edited a number of Papers like "Social Science ,and public administration, He has also published a number of Book Chapters in various Books.

Dr. Murlidhar Mandal
Guest Lecture Political Science
J.M.S. College ,Munger, Tilka Manjhi
Bhagalpur University,Bihar INDIA

Acknowledgement

For bringing the Book to the final shape I can never forget the involvement and concern of my Supervisor, Prof. (Dr) Roma Mitra, Former H.O.D., Dept. of Political Science, T.M. Bhagalpur University, Bhagalpur. I do not have more words to express my gratitude towards her. I pray, she has a peaceful days ahead.

I, with a sense of gratitude, express my indebtedness to my parents Sri Baital Pd. Mandal and Tara Devi for their inspiration and greater concern for my higher education. I am also thankful to my wife - Priti Devi ,My Son - .Aditya Sen and My brothers- Manmohan and Murari

Dr. Murlidhar Mandal

Guest Lecture Political Science

J.M.S. College ,Munger, Tilka Manjhi

Bhagalpur University,Bihar INDIA

PREFACE

You perceive a thing as you are and not as they are. With this ideas behind the study was planned to get things. From the eyes, of the leadership of selected *Panchayats in Naugachia Sub-division of Bhagalpur District in regard to the affairs around the latest brand of Panchayat System under the Panchayati Raj Scheme of things. As we know the constitution has always visualised the P.R.I.S. as the unit of Slf Govt. and later on as the Institution of Self Govt. As a historical measure the 73rd Amendment emphasises on Panchayats to be institution itself, rather than being units merely. The onus of shaping out Panchayats in its new avtar naturally fallson the leadership unless the leaders play an active role things would hardly take an appropriate shape. How far the present set up of leadership has been able to take an appropriate shape. How far the present set up of leadership has been able to take things a far has been the basic concern of the present doctoral thesis.*

For bringing the thesis to the final shape I can never forget the involvement and concern of my Supervisor, Prof. (Dr) Roma Mitra, Former H.O.D., Dept. of Political Science, T.M. Bhagalpur University, Bhagalpur. I do not have more words to express my gratitude towards her. I pray, she has a peaceful days ahead.

I am also thankful to Dr. Manisha Laheri, the Co-supervisor, who was quite helpful in preparation of the manuscript.

I also owe to Prof. (Dr) Menka Sahay, the Present II.O.D., Dept. of Political Science, T.M. Bhagalpur University, Bhagalpur and to all my teachers in the Dept. who were equally helpful as and when their guidance was sought for.

I, with a sense of gratitude, express my indebtedness to my parents Sri Baital Pd. Mandal and Tara Devi for their inspiration and greaterconcern for my higher education. I am also thankful to my brothers- Manmohan and Murari.

I will fail in my duty if I do not mention above the cooperation I got from my friend Nutan Kumari, who was always a source of strength for me while doing the thesis.

I also feel like acknowledging those respondents who though not knowledgeable to the desired extent were forthright in acceding their ignorance also.

I acknowledge in good grace the skill of the Computer printer Smt. Shobha Lal, 'Lal Computers', Tilkamanjhi Hat, Bhagalpur and also her efficiency in printing and typing.

Dr. Murlidhar Mandal

<table>
<tr><td>CHAPTER NO.</td><td>CONTENTS</td><td>PAGE NO.</td></tr>
</table>

INTRODUCTION

PANCHAYATS THEN AND NOW

In India Panchayat system has been the part of social life since times immemorial. During the Vedic period as the story goes, Panchayats were the administrative unit for village administration which was blessed with complete empowerment as if it had the Divine support. People believed in the system unequivocally so its authority remained unchallenged and non-controversial for long-long time. Panchayats held very important position during the Ramayan and the Mahabharat periods. Similarly during the Buddhist and Mauryan periods, Panchayats or Gram Sanghs were entrusted to run the village administration of Republics. Muslim rulers also did not disturb the Panchayat system. However, during the Mughal period Panchayats ceased to be of any administrative importance whatsoever. During the period villages were mostly ruled by landlords or their agents. What ever changes might have been there, Panchayats continued to exist as a system of some significance. The main force sustaining the system has been the society itself. Respectable leaders in the villages normally used to be he king-pins of Panchayats and their words regarded as "gospel truth".[1] This way we can very much see that Panchayat at village level existed in India since time immemorial. Though the present Panchayat system has no direct bearing of the traditional system of Panchayat that existed in the ancient and medieval period much of its inspiration and faith people have in it today are derived from the system that flourished in the past. The Panchayat of today a statutory and elected body, responsible for the development of the village was established in this country in the later part of the 19th century.

With the establishment of the British Rule in India, Panchayats were given least importance in the administration which, in turn, led to the disruption in the village community life. However, after the year 1857, rural self Govt. as an idea received considerable governmental attention and little bit of importance. However, the year 1882 opened a new chapter in the growth of Local Self Govt. (L.S.G). The Resolution of Lord Ripon, who subsequently came to be regarded as the father of the concept of L.S.G. in India, was a positive attempt to reconsider the revival of village institutions. Accordingly Panchayats and Local Boards were set up in the provinces of the British India. Further in 1907, the British Govt. appointed the Decentralisation Commission to recommend measures for the revival of L.S.G.[2] The Commission observed that the system of L.S.G. should begin from village level instead of from District level. The Commission also insisted that the tehsil or taluka boards should exist to fill the gap between the village Panchayats and District Boards. Before the introduction of Montague-Chlemsford constitutional reforms the Govt. of India passed a resolution in May 1918, emphasizing the need for separate legislation to accelerate the development of Panchayats.

During the struggle for freedom the revival of Panchayat was accepted as an article of faith. Mahatma Gandhi wanted to build the entire policy on the foundation of Village Swaraj. He also wrote :

"My idea of Village Swaraj is that it is a complete republic, independent of its neighbours for its own vital wants, and yet interdependent for many others in which dependence is a necessity." Further Gandhiji believed that decentralization was essential of the ideal democracy to enable each individual to participate in the decision making and its implementation process. Democracy was the embodiment of real freedom to manage its own affairs. His concept of decentralisation implies the basic principle of self-sufficiency in respect of the basic needs of man.[3]

After attainment of freedom in 1947 the question before the country was : what should be the administrative structure of the country? There was the thinking of Gandhi himself who thought that Panchayats were an instrument of mass politics for a net work of such rural organisation functioning in the village without any connection with the Govt. will be the true foundation of civil revolt.

Independent India, as such, was suddenly faced with problems that were myriad. The Congress Party which came to rule over the country was faced with problems that needed immediate attention. The political dismemberment of the country gave rise to serious communal riots and refugee problems. Food situation was alarming. After these problems were eventually tackled the country had to come to grip with the intractable problems of poverty since mass poverty could be eliminated only through mass participation, there were urgent need to revive and refashioning institutions through which mass could be brought to the vortex of modernization.

While grappling with such enormous and complicated national. Problems Gandhiji exposed his mind stressing the need for revival of Panchayat system. Quoting what Gandhi had himself meant from its revival- he said "in my view "establishment of true democracy is possible only through a non-violent society. In such a society the poorest and the weakest. Persons will get an opportunity for his fullest development- there will be neither communal hatred nor any feeling of high and low. Our democracy will be based on social justice under which freedom will grow from below and every village will be administered through its own Panchayat "Indian independence" added Gandhi" must begin at the bottom. Thus every village will be a republic or a Panchayat, having full powers. It follows, therefore that every village has to be self sustained and capable of managing its affairs even to the extent of defending itself against the whole world. Further he said, if ever there is to be a republic of every village in India, then I claim for my picture, in which the last is equal to the first, or in other words, no one is to be the first and none the last."

Respecting the views expressed by Gandhijee the makers of the Indian constitution laid down in the Directive Principles of the State Policy outlining the future set up of Panchayats- "the State shall take steps to organize village Panchayats and endow them with such powers and authority as may be necessary to enable them to function as unit of self-Govt."

The National Planning Commission which came into existence in March 1950 to establish a welfare State also favoured revival of Panchayat system for village development since more than 80 percent of the Indian population lived in villages. With this purpose in view the Planning Commission released a draft outline to the nation in July 1951 which included the justification for wide spread public participation in development planning. The Draft said : "Planning in a democratic country is a social process in which, in some part, every citizen should have the opportunity to participate. It expressed the conviction that the crucial function in organizing the community for action is leadership not only at the top but at all levels. For the emergence of local level leadership Panchayat system was thus essentially required to be revived.

The First Five Year Plan also felt that unless a village agency could assume the responsibility and initiative for developing the resources of the village, it would be difficult to make a marked impression on rural life, for only a village organisation representing the community as a whole can provide the necessary leadership.

Enormity and urgency of the rural problems facing the developing countries which had come out of the colonial rule led to the creation of plethora of new institutions- political, economic, social and administrative. People's institutions become instrumental in accelerating the pace of development where as the bureaucratic machinery alone is considered inadequate for the task of nation building.[4] Bureaucracy any where plays a more static role; thrust and dynamism required for development can come best from non-bureaucratic sources. To promote political development and social justice people's institutions are to be created.[5] Establishing and sustaining viable institutions should be critical concern of modern political elite, planners and administrators in the developing countries, since this is a measure element in their operating strategy.[6] Therefore, local organisation is a necessary if not sufficient condition for the accelerated rural development.[7]

In India, during the initial phase of independence and in view of the enormity of socio-economic problems as have also been stated in the chapter, the Govt. first of all started Grow More Food Campaign for achieving self-sufficiency in food matters. The campaign however, failed to deliver the goods. The Second Project of the Govt. came in the form of Extension services organisation in 19052. Community Development Blocks were created in every state to provide a standard unit within the District for the purposes of administering the development programmes. These Community Development Blocks through officers assigned to them were to administer the development programmes concerning agriculture, animal husbandry, education, health, social welfare, co-operation and small scale industries. Such a recourse to development was taken in an attempt to secure the people's participation in the execution of development programmes for without such participation their acceptance of the sponsored schemes remained uncertain. Besides so much of development responsibilities the National Extension Service were also required to stimulate local initiative, to promote community activities and also to see that the vast unutilized energy in village is harvested to work for the benefit of a part or whole of the community.

Prior to the series of innovative measures to promote development in rural areas through out the country, Panchayat as a statutory system was already there through state enactments. In Bihar too Panchayat, in modern sense, came into being as early as in 1947 through the Bihar Act.

The Second Five Year Plan envisaged a Panchayat as responsible for village development keeping transformation of social and economic life of rural areas as its goal of development. It lays that "rural progress depend entirely on the existence of an active organisation in the village which can bring all the people, including the weaker sections into common programmes to be carried out with the assistance of administration." To achieve this objective the Second Five Year Plan entailed the Panchayats to perform

  a) Civic

  b) developmental,

  c) land management,

  d) Land Reforms, and

  e) Judicial Functions.[8]

If reorganizing Panchayats formed part of national policy of securing people's participation in rural reconstruction programmes, the Community Development Ministry of the Govt. of India introduced a new system of extension Service Organisation in 1952 itself taking care of those factors responsible for the failure of Grow More Food Campaign started in the country immediately after Indian Independence Community Development Blocks were created in every state to provide a standard unit of administration within the district for the purpose of administering the development programmes.

The basic idea underlying the movement was intensive development aiming at reaching every family in the country side and at securing coordinated development of rural life as a whole in order to secure local cooperation, to stimulate local initiative, to promote community activities and also to see that the vast unutilized energy in village is harvested to work for the benefit for a part or whole of the community. The new experiment in the form of a national movement was expected to be based on the foundation of village Self Govt, i.e. Panchayat as an Institution. Every effort of development, therefore was to be directed towards building up a free and vigorous life not only through Panchayats but also through multipurpose societies.

The Community Development Movement could not succeed on desired lines. It utterly failed to revitalize Panchayats which had fallen in desuetude, an important task tagged with the movement. To press into service the community initiative and participation there was no basic change in the existing situation of the Panchayats through out the country. Bihar was not an exception Mukhia both as a person and an institution was very much there to hob-hob but not akin to his/her accountability towards making Panchayat as an effective instrument of social change and economic management Panchayats which was supposed to be a unit of Govt. at the village as also recommended in the Second Five Year Plan could not grow at all on the desired line. Adih Doctor observed "Panchayats have done very little with their statutory powers- that even when they are formally responsible for preparing plans "It is the official who did the job and most of the Panchayats restricted their activities to municipal function like street lighting, water supply. In general, village Panchayats seldom meet and when they do it is mostly to conduct regular business such as selecting office-bearer and the like."[9]

The Committee on Plan Project set up a study team. The team which subsequently came to be known as Balwant Rai Mehta submitted its Report in Nov. 1957. The team's observation about the role of village Panchayats in the development matters in their report is worth mentioning. "The available information indicates that possibly not more than 10 percent of the total number of Panchayat are functioning effectively, roughly one-half are average and the remaining about 40% are working unsatisfactorily ... The actual performance of Panchayats is generally limited to making arrangements for sanitation, conservancy, construction and repair of fair weather Roads, provision of domestic water supply and street lighting. Even these simple and elementary civic functions are not being performed with a degree of efficiency over large areas ... only small number of Panchayats, those situated within or near the Block areas have shown a zeal for development activities on any appreciable scale.[10] Explaining financial crisis facing Panchayats the study Team on Plan Project observed : "The Panchayats are generally handicapped for want of adequate financial resources to meet the growing expenditure on local programmes of development. It is evident that without financial assistance from the State Govt. many Panchayats can't continue their existence. It would appear from the available data that the majority of working Panchayats over large areas have an annual income not exceeding Rs. 500/- from all sources including Govt. Subsidy Deducting the cost of small establishments maintained by the Panchayats on account of pay of the Secretary who is whole time or part time in many cases, conservancy staff, contingencies and contributions for the up-keep of Nyay Panchayats, very little is left for constructive and welfare activities. There are three major aspects of the problems relating to finance; inadequate resources allotted to Panchayats under the Acts, a general reluctance to make use of the existing resources and general inefficiency in tax administration.

Not all Panchayats levy even compulsory taxes and fewer collected them with any degree of efficiency. In Bihar, Orissa and Madhya Pradesh it is reliably learnt that the collections do not exceed 25-30%. In many cases Panchas and Sarpanchas are among the defaulters. The complaints of discrimination in assessment are fairly common and in a few cases a deliberative victimization. The assessment lists are not periodically revised. There is general aversion to adopt coercive measures, which, it is feared, will make the Panchayats unpopular. It is well to bear in mind that the general failure to assess and collect the various taxes and fees has wider repercussions. It creates an atmosphere unfavourable to the growth of the Panchayats."[11]

Ultimately the study team recommended the creation of ".... a single representative and vigorous institution to take charge of all aspects of development work in rural areas. Such a body if created, has to be statutory, elective comprehensive in its duties and functions equipped with necessary executive machinery and in possession of adequate resources. It must have the powers to make mistake, and it must also receive guidance, which will help it to avoid making mistakes. In the ultimate analysis it must be an instrument of expression of local people's will in regard to their local development. The jurisdiction of the proposed body should be neither so large as to defeat the very purpose for which it is created nor so small in area, population and financial resources to carry out all these functions. Obviously too, the next higher body will have to function with and through the Panchayats as far as possible, for the very reasons which we have considered are that this institution should be identical in extent with NES. Block, the Tehsil or Taluka, the sub-division (when this consists of more than one Tehsil or the district. Many of the districts are at present too large in area and population. And people, particularly expected too, in our circumstances can not be expected to take a personal sacrifice for common institution at the local Govt. levels unless these are small enough for their influence to demonstrably accept."

The Block, on the other hand, offers an area large enough for functions which village Panchayats can not perform and yet small enough to attract the interest and service of the residents. There is the further factor that some of the Blocks are already working as the development units and have been equipped for this purpose with adequate personnel in different fields. It is true that there will have to be effective coordination at a higher level (the machinery for which we will discuss later); but we are of the view that the most efficient and useful arrangement in this regard is to have an elected self-governing institution which jurisdiction would be coterminous with a Development Block.

If the body is to function with any vigour, initiative and success the Govt. will have to devolve upon it, within the body's jurisdiction reserving to itself the function of guidance, supervision and higher planning and where necessary providing for extra funds. The broad-objectives, the general pattern and the measure of financial, technical and supervisory assistance available have to be worked out by the states, but it is for the people's representatives assisted by the Govt. staff to work out and execute details of the plan. The fixation of targets should, therefore, be a joint responsibility of the state on the one hand and the local representatives on the other. The responsibility has to be clearly defined but firmly interlinked."[12]

Another important and revolutionary measure recommended by the study team was to bring democratic decentralisation in local administration. The team was of the definite view that the time had arrived in India when central and State Govts. must repose greater faith and trust the people for their own welfare. They also suggested that basic unit of Local Govt. for purpose of development should be the village Panchayat. Maximum of power should be devolved and delegated to this body for implementation of the Community Development Programme which falls within the territorial jurisdiction of the village.

The National Development Committee of India accepted the basic recommendations of the study Team in 1958. To bring home the meaning of Local Govt. to the people in India and to make it more intimate to the ordinary man, indigenous name of ancient or traditional organisation i.e. Panchayati Raj was given to the new units of Local Govt. which was to be based on decentralisation. Explaining its implications Chetakar Jha has observed "It is a great turning point in the history of Local Self Government in India. Apart from the fact that Local Self Governing institutions are coming to have economic functions the movement of Panchayati Raj is an experiment in new ideas in regard to the structure and other aspects of Local Govt. System. The distinction between Local Govt. institutions and the Local Self Governing institutions which have so far characterized our system is getting blurred and may, perhaps, fade away in days to come. The Panchayati Raj Movement is pregnant with enormous possibilities of far reaching consequences. The entires administrative landscape is undergoing political change."[13]

The Historic Congress Session at Bhavanagar in early 1961 gave a mandate to all states to speed up the legislation and implement the programme of democratic decentralisation. The Govt. of India also laid the following basic guide-lines for Panchayati Raj.[14]

1. It should be a three tier structure of Local Self Governing bodies from the village to the District, the body being organically linked.

2. There should be a genuine transfer of power and responsibility to them.

3. Adequate resources should be transferred to the new bodies to enable them to discharge these responsibilities.

4. All development programmes at these levels should be channeled through these bodies.

5. The system evolved should be such as will facilitate further devolution and dispersal of power and responsibilities in the future.

The Govt. of Bihar appointed a Committee to consider the future set up of District Boards in Bihar under the Chairmanship of Maqbool Ahmad. The Committee in its Report observed : We also agree with the view expressed in the regard by the Balwant Rai Mehta Committee that the existing district boards will not be able to discharge their responsibilities we feel that rural development and rural welfare are possible only with personal initiative and local zeal. We therefore, agree with the recommendations of the Balwant Rai Mehta Committee that there should also be a Panchayat Samiti at the Block level where it will be easier to coordinate the work of rural development of the village. Panchayats, as generally a Block comprises about 16 to 24 village Panchayats."[15]

Following the recommendations of the above study Team the Govt. of Bihar enacted the Bihar Panchayat Samitis and Zila Parishads Act, 1961.

The authors and planners of Panchayati Raj (PR), ever since its inception, have been taking sustained and continuous interest in the evaluation of its performance to ensure that it was to tune with their expectations about its capabilities.

The Bihar Panchayat Raj Act, 1947, and The Bihar Panchayat Samitis and Zila Parishad Act, 1961 had undergone modification from time to time. After about a decade of its working, a realisation of the futility of easy optimism of its capabilities dawned upon the State Govt. and persuaded to give serious thoughts to bring about a major reorganisation of the whole gamut of Panchayati Raj in the seventies such as

a) Sub Committee on Amendment to the Bihar Panchayat Raj Act, 1947 and Rules under the Chairmanship of S.K. Bage.

b) Sub-Committee on Amendment to the Bihar Panchayat Samitis and Zila Parishads Act, 1961 and Rules under the Chairmanship of Lal Singh Tyagi.

Initially, designed as a politico-administrative set up to make up for the short comings of the Community Development (CD) Programmes, Panchayati Raj grew over a period of years as a vehicle of popular participation in the development of rural area. "Indeed, since the inaugurations of the C.D. Programme, people's participation has come to be equated with the doctrine of development. The C.D. Programme emphasised the need of creating local authorities, where they were non-existent and strengthening those which were wek.[16]

Since the introduction of the statutory Panchayat, the concept of its duties has undergone modifications. Initially it was required to perform, in main, the municipal and regulatory functions. Under the impact of Planning and Community Development Panchayat has been conceived as the appropriate agency of socio-economic advance in the rural areas. Accordingly, in Bihar, the Act of 1947 was amended in 1959 to add some new functions pertaining to agricultural development. The Act of 1947 classifies Panchayat duties into two broad categories

1. Compulsory duties covering 19 items, and

2. Supplementary duties covering 29 items.[17]

However owing the scarce finance, ill equipped leadership and personnel, apathy of the people towards Panchayat, inadequate assistance and guidance from the Govt. etc, the Panchayat has virtually ceased to fulfill its compulsory and supplementary duties.[18]

Now the point is : How did things look up when Panchayati Raj bodies started function? "There were hardly a few states where Panchayati Raj institutions got the state patronage and were pushed off by the state powers. In majority of states they were almost stemmed and immeasurably constrained to take off.[19] Reviewing their performance Ashoka Mehta Committee (1978) remarked "Corruption, efficiency, scant regard for procedures, political interference in day today administration, motivated power concentration all these have seriously limited the utility of Panchayati Raj for the average villager. Next came the G.V.K. Rao Committee in 1985 and L.M. Singhvi in 1986. The Rao Report had observed that Panchayati Raj institutions were sabotaged by bureaucracy and vested local interests in most places. They gathered the impression that both these elements acted in connivance with legislators and M.Ps. from the respective areas with the notion that Panchayat Raj was a still born child. For Rajni Kothari " Panchayati Raj itself being reduced to gimmick."[20]

Speaking in terms of Bihar where Panchayati Raj scheme was introduced phase wise, these institutions were hardly given the scope to act up to themselves. The scheme remained sandwiched between political leaders and bureaucrats nexus. The amount of restraints imposed on the functioning of these institutions under the State Act coupled with callousness on the part of the bureaucracy apparently strangulated Panchayati Raj bodes in its very infancy. Irregular elections to these bodies had been the common feature- where there had been no election to these bodies. Way back since 1978. Besides, malicious design of the State Govt. against the spirit of Panchayati Raj have also come to light. The Bihar Panchayati Raj (Amendment) Bill 1991 is an illustration. The Bill was brought in for legislation before the 73rd amendment of the constitution came to effect. However, the provisions contained in the proposed Bill reflected the intent of the Govt. which will be evident from the excerpt of the Bill. "The Govt. was empowered to nominate Mukhias and Sarpanch as well as the members of the executive bodies and Gram Kutcheries at village level till the next election."[21] The Bill of course did not see the light of the day.

The system was not only weakened from outside. The insiders were also equally responsible for not allowing the institution to grow on the desired lines. We will just illustrate certain developments that took place in the process of its working.

For the sake of effective functioning Panchayats were divided into three different wings : Deliberative, Executive and Judiciary. The deliberative wing was the Gram Sabha, a statutory body consisting of the entire adult population within its area. Statutorily the Gram Sabha had to be the Supreme Decision Making Body. The basic purpose behind its prominence was to promote the cause of participatory democracy besides being an attempt to evoke popular enthusiasm of the entire rural population. Notwithstanding such a pious notion Gram Sabha did hardly meet and if it met at all it was just by way of formalities and never with the seriousness of the purpose.

The other wing, the Executive wing consisted of the Mukhia and other members partly nominated and partly elected. The Committee was statutorily expected to carry on the task assigned to it by the Deliberative wing. In the event of Deliberative wing having pushed behind the scene the Executive Committee also miserably failed to establish its viability. Gradually, it became perfunctory on papers, its meetings were convened at regular intervals but it could hardly transact a business for want of quorum which always was lacking. If at all the meeting was held it was more or less of routine importance and administrative works occupied most of their time.[22]

With deliberative and executive wing having ceased to be meaningfully operative, Panchayat became virtually 'one man show' and virtually defunct. The administrative and regulative jobs initially assigned to Panchayats eventually turned to be the personal accountability of Mukhias who by virtue of their acceptance by the local administration put their heads and shoulders above their collegues in the Panchayat reducing Panchayat as an institution almost jobless, " Panchayats were intended to be development agencies but utmost they became the field extension unit of the State Govt. Because of the administrative and regulative tasks assigned to the Panchayats they had taken up only a few functions of obligatory nature out of the big list provided in the Act. There was every truth in the observation of the study of Team on Panchayati Raj Finance that there were Panchayats who were not discharging the minimum obligatory functions. Even the basic civic amenities like safe drinking water supply sanitation and conservancy were no provided to the community.[23] The only difference on can notice between the (traditional Panchayats) Panchayats of pre Panchayati era with those of the post era was degree of importance that had been attached to them under the banner of Panchayati Raj. The reality of the situation was that under the new system Panchayats in general had been degraded to a status of comparative unimportance and inferiority. Ram K, Veppa, analyzing the prevailing trend observed "Although the new Act provides some assistance to Panchayats which will help their proper functioning it is unlikely that Panchayats will develop into the lusty children they are expected to grow. Considering the present situation it is feared they will continue to remain the weakest link in the three tier pattern, although in theory they form the basis on which the entire edifice of Panchayati

Raj rests. No new source of revenue have been assigned to them nor is their dependence on Govt. grants likely to be reduced."[24]

Panchayats role in planning of village production plan had only remained on paper. The expectations that Panchayats will be effective instruments of economic progress and social change remained a myth only. Left to themselves with no outside impetus, they miserably failed to move a step forward depending on their own resources what so ever they were. In Bihar they were virtually non-existent if they existed at all it was without self-entity.

Besides all these, the pivotal role assigned to the Panchayat Samitis under the Bihar Panchayat Samitis and Zila Parishads Act, 1961 was squarely responsible for shadowing the Panchayats which had to languish terribly.

The statutory Panchayat system was supposed to be endowed with dynamic leadership by throwing an opportunity to the masses to challenge the established traditional leaders through electoral processes.   But it had not to be. Contrary to such expectations Panchayat system became the sheet of powers for mostly those who had been erst while zamindars and who through the office of Panchayat sought to compensate for their losses particularly social. Taking advantage of democracy to do undemocratic things was the basic characteristics of such leadership. It was their monopoly to behave in their own terms.

Panchayats were also expected to turn the Community Development Programmes into people's programmes with Govt's. participation. Experiences showed it that people's participation was hard to secure so long as the programmes continued to be Govt. sponsored and failed miserably to associate people with the formulation and implementation of programmes.

Summing up we may say that Panchayati Raj institutions in Bihar were hardly given the scope to act up to themselves. The concept remained sandwiched between political leaders and bureaucrat nexus. The amount of restraints imposed on these institutions under the State Act, coupled with callousness on the part of the bureaucracy ultimately strangulated Panchayati Raj institutions in its very infancy. In other words, Panchayati Raj institutions, particularly statutory village Panchayat suffered all infirmities right since the day the very concept of Panchayati Raj was mooted out. However, with the 73rd amendment of the Indian Constitution which basically seeks to bring both democracy and devolution of powers through Panchayats all over the country things have started looking up.

Panchayats can't be arbitrarily suspended or dissolved any more. No one will be able to take away the power responsibilities and finances devolved upon the Panchayats. It is now believed the constitutional measures will prove to be a land mark for the proper growth of Panchayati System. However, in between the constitutional measures and the desired efficiency of the system there is a very important element which we can't afford to miss. It is the leadership in the form of elected representatives for the institution. The socio-economic development of any rural community depends to a great extent on the quality of leadership unless the leaders play an active role progress in right direction will be impossible. Hence the Panchayat leadership which are instrumental for the development of rural population through its active involvement becomes the "gap-closer" between the bureaucracy and the masses thereby filling up a vast organisational gap. Further, the leadership are supposed to mediate between tradition and modernity and play an educative role through broadening the range and deepening the reach of participatory process by accelerating the pace of modernization. They are also expected to instill in the people a sense of partnership in development programme and seek their cooperation and support in their implementation. Further more, by effective planning and implementation, it will utilize the available resources by taking into account the local interests. Further more, the leadership will mobilize local resources in the delivery of intents and services. The leadership will communicate the requirements of the people in voicing their concern at higher rungs of administration. This sort of communication and interaction would positively facilitate the strengthening of the administrative accountability and responsiveness in the sphere of socio-economic development.

With the 73rd amendment and subsequent passage of the Bihar Panchayati Raj Act, 1993 it has been ensured that the real power goes to the Panchayati Raj institutions. In the given situation the leadership is expected to play a much greater role in development of the people. Now they have to ensure that powers vested in these institutions are effectively utilised so that they become vibrant institutions- performing necessary developmental, regulatory and general administrative functions. Specific responsibilities have been entrusted to the Panchayats to prepare plans for economic development and social justice in respect of matters listed in the XIth schedule of the constitution. Panchayats have thus been called upon to shoulder the responsibilities of 29 departments relating directly to the people's welfare.

In Bihar Panchayati Raj institutions have been reorganized with the elections in the year 2001. The elections were held after a long gap of 23 years, the last one held in the year 1978. The reorganized Panchayats are not only well equipped with powers and resources under the constitutional decree they have now a new set up of leadership quite different not only socially but also temperamentally compared to the previous one. How do they find their job they have been called upon to shoulder is the basic point that hovers round the entire study. Besides, how things have started taking shape under their leadership will naturally be a point of discussion ... Leadership know what is best for the people and not the people themselves. Leaders have to be not only active but also pro-active depending on the demand of the situation.

Keeping in view of all these aspects into considerations the study has been so designed so as to enable us to be aware of leaders' perception in regard to their various institutional responsibilities they have been called upon to shoulder. In the process of investigation the constraints they have to encounter in performing their job will also be taken note of. We should never forget that one of the major tasks of P.R.I.S. has been providing selection of universe assistance to the weaker sections of the society. This has also been the objective of the various Five Year Plans and C.D. Programmes. the successive Five Year Plan underlined the need for equitable distribution of gains from development and also stressed people's participation in the programmes of development. About the Panchayati Raj it was even stated in the Third Five Year Plan that the assistance rendered to the weaker sections of the village community by the P.R.I.S. will be periodically evaluated for further assistance.[25]

The challenge of rural poverty cannot be met without the active involvement of PRIS. Panchayats are being looked upon as a means to achieve socio-economic transformation of our rural societies.

It is, however, generally believed that the socio-economic benefits through Panchayati Raj have not gone sufficiently to the weaker sections of the village community who are oppressed and suppressed. Analyzing the performance of Panchayati Raj in India, Iqbal Narain observes that the system of democratic decentralisation has in fact, deepened economic disparities by its inability to check the flow of developmental benefits to those who are socially, economically and politically dominant (CAS. quoted in Arora, 1979). Late Mrs. Gandhi, in the message sent by her on the occasion of Sixth National Sammelan of All India Panchayat Parishad held in Delhi in March 1973 reiterated that "we shall not be able to achieve progress and stability in our villages or indeed in the country as a whole, unless the groups which have so long been kept out of the political process, economic power and social prestige are not brought fully into the main stream." (1973 : 13).

While aiming at the many faceted development it has to be ensured that the fruits of development have generally gone to the less privileged sections of society. This problem had drawn the attention of the study group on the welfare of the weaker sections (under the Chairmanship of Jai Prakash Narain) as far back as in 1960 itself. This study group very emphatically stated that "the whole bias of Panchayati Raj has to be towards the weaker sections of the community. Added to these, "the Panchayati Raj leaders drawn out of the local soil will be more in touch with local social ethic, rather than the national "modernizing" ethic and even if a few local leaders are able to break away from their "grass roots" affiliations and accept "modern" cultural and social norms, the political necessity of contesting elections will force them to take a stand point more sympathetic to local ethos and ethics as against the edicts and enactments of national leaders and legislators.[25]

METHODOLOGY

All the seven blocks falling within Naugachia sub-division viz. Gopalpur, Narayanpur, Bihpur, Rangra, Kharik, Naugachia and Ismailpur formed the universe of the study. One Panchayat in each block was selected for the purpose of interview with the Panchayat leadership. Leadership for us comprised of both Mukhia and the ward members.

The table below furnishes leadership strength in Naugachia sub-division Panchayat wise.

Table 1

Block	Panchayat	Mukhia	Ward Members		Total
			Male	Female	
Gopalpur	Dimha Gopalpur	1	9	5	14+1
Narayanpur	Jaipur Chaurhar	1	9	4	13+1
Bihpur	Lattipur Dakshin	1	9	4	13+1
Rangra	Tintenga Uttri	1	9	4	13+1
Kharik	Tulsipur	1	9	5	14+1
Naugachia	Jagatpur	1	9	5	14+1
Ismailpur		1	9	4	13+1

94+7= 101

Total number of Leaders = 101

N = 101.

SELECTION of Respondents

The scale of selection of sample unit remained almost standardized in each of the Panchayat of all the seven blocks under Naugachia sub-division. In terms of leadership rank of our respondents- each Mukhia, and all the Ward members of the Panchayats under investigation formed part of or sample respondents.

RESEARCH TOOLS

For collection of data we had a structured questionnaire to be administered upon the above categories of respondents. We also had to take recourse to secondary sources to the extent it was required within the framework of the study.

NOTES AND REFERENCES

1. Report of the Decentralisation Commission of India, Para 699, 1909.

2. Report of the Decentralisation Commission upon India, Para 699, 1909.

3. M.K. Gandhi " Panchayati Raj" compiled by R.K. Prabha Navjivan Publishing House, (1952), pp. 11-12.

4. Milton & Esman: The Politics of Development Administration, p. 59, 1994.

5. G. Ram Reddy : Panchayati Raj and Rural Development in Andhra Pradesh- India (1974),p. 88, Cornel University.

6. Milton & Esman, Op.Cit. p. 143.

7. Report of the Committee on Panchayati Raj Institutions, Here in after cited as Ashoka Mehta Committee Report.

8. V. Shivaling Prasad : Panchayat and Development- (1981) p. 9- Light and Life Publishers.

9. Adih Doctor- Studies in Indian Democracy, (1965), Allied Publishers, 0. 375.

10. Section- 2, Vol. I of the Report of the Study Team of Committee on Plan Project (1957), Committee for Plan Project.

11. Sec. 3.3, Vol. I of the Report of the Study Team on Plan Project (1957), Committee for Plan Project.

12. Sec. 3, Vol. I of the Report of the Study Team on Plan Project (1957), Committee for Plan Project.

13. Chctakar Jha : Indian Local Self Govt. (1969), p. 30, Novelty and Co.

14. Shiviah: Dilemmas of Democratic Politics in India (1966),p. 95, Manak Tolas, Bombay.

15. Report of the Committee constituted by the State Govt. to consider the future set up of District Boards in Bihar (1960), p. 12.

16. Govt. of Bihar, Directorate of Panchayati Raj, Patna, 1973 (Hindi-Mimeo).

17. Sec. 14 and 15 of the Bihar Panchayati Raj Act, 1947.

18. Haridwar Rai and Awadhesh Prasad "Reorganizing Panchayati Raj in Bihar- A critique of the Reform Proposal"- I.I.P.A. Vol. XXI, No. 1, Jan. March, 1975.

19. G.N. Thakur, " Panchayati Raj- Hopesand Despair" in Rural Development in India (Ed) Anmol Prakashan, p. 202.

20. The Times of India, dt. 7.6.1963.

21. G.N. Thakur, Op.Cit., pp. 202-03.

22. G.N. Thakur, Unpublished Ph.D. Thesis entitled "Working of Zila Parishads and Panchayat Samitis in Bihar" Submitted to the Bihar University (1975), p. 231.

23. Report of the Study Team on Panchayati Raj finance ec. 3.13 (1963), Govt. of India, Ministry of Community Development and Cooperation.

24.   Ram K. Veppa; Indian Journal of Public Administration, Oc. Dec. 1964, p. 692.

25.   Govt. of India (1961 : 338-39).

BACKGROUND OF LEADER (ELECTED LEADERS AT PANCHAYAT LEVEL)

India has made its choice in favour of treating political participation as an integral part of development. It has adopted a democratic political system based on competitive participation of citizens in the management of public affairs. Further, the importance of citizens participation in development process has not only been recognised but repeatedly emphasised. And, in fact, Panchayati Raj was born of this concern. The goal of citizen participation was built into the administrative organisation for developmental programmes as back as co-immunity development movement was launched after Indian independence. The three-tier administrative set-up the village and the local authority, the State Govt. and the Central Govt. has provided enough scope for not only people's participation but also a greater network of rural leadership to emerge.

He ensure also tried to that the State Govts. decentralised substantial powers to them so that those who sought to manage them not only satisfied their ego but were also in a position to do some tangible service to the community. These institutions, were, therefore, deemed to serve the double purpose of sharing with the State and Central Govts. the responsibility of developing the country-side and also of absorbing the overflow of the new, emerging leadership. "Our experience of early sixties does reveal to us that these institutions had begun to serve both these purposes, reasonably well. With their inspiration and effort an impressive degree of local effort had been mobilised for development activities. At the same time, the new, young and enthusiastic leaders took pride in serving these institutions and they would mostly treat their membership of Panchayati Raj as a useful training ground for the high forums at the state and central levels. The record of performance of these institutions (at a stage when they enjoyed both autonomy of action and substantial powers) has by no means been less impressive.[1]

One of the major tasks of Panchayati Raj (PR) activities since its inception has been providing assistance to the weaker sections of the society. Similar has been the objective of the various Five Year Plans and Community Development Programmes. The successive Five Year Plans underlined the need for equitable distribution of gains from development and also stressed people's participation in the programmes of development. About the Panchayati Raj it was even stated in the Third Five Year Plan that the assistance rendered to the weaker sections of the village community by the Panchayati Raj institutions will be periodically evaluated for further assistance.[2]

The challenge of rural poverty cannot be met without the active involvement of PRIS. Panchayats are looked upon as a means to achieve socio-economic transformation of the rural societies. It is generally believed that the socio-economic benefits through Panchayati Raj have not sufficiently gone to the weaker sections of the village community who are still oppressed and suppressed. In the depth analysis of the performance of Panchayati Raj in India, Iqbal Narain observes that the system of democratic decentralisation has, in fact deepened economic disparities by its inability to check the flow of developmental benefits to those who are socially, economically and politically dominant (CAS quoted in Aurora, 1979). Late Mrs. Indira Gandhi, in her message on the occasion of the IXth National Sammelan of All India Panchayat Parishad in Delhi in March 1973 reiterated that "we shall not be able to achieve progress and stability in our villages or indeed in the country as a whole, unless the groups which have so long been kept out of the political process, economic power and social prestige, are now brought fully into the mainstream." (1973, 13).

While aiming at the many faceted development it has to be ensured that the fruits of development accrue more and more to the less privileged sections of the community. It is widely felt that the fruits of economic development have generally gone to the richer sections of the society. This problem had drawn the attention of the study group on the welfare of the weaker sections (under the Chairmanship of Jai Prakash Narain) as back as in 1960 itself. This study group very emphatically stated that "the whole bias of Panchayati Raj has to be towards the weaker sections of the community.

It is in this context that we have to analyse the leadership pattern that has emerged from period to period. Leadership pattern determines that ability to cope with the tasks assigned to the PRIS. We have had varieties of leadership who served their personal interests at the cost of those who actually needed their sympathy and patronage.

A few lines in regard to leadership in literary sense will not be irrelevant.

"One who leads is a leader" is the general definition of a leader. Leadership is the relationship between an individual and a group built around some common interest and behaving in a manner directed or determined by him. The common interest may include material ends, factional, economic, technical, political interests, etc. This relationship arises only where a group follows an individual by free choice and on positive or more or less rational grounds rather than under coercion or in response to blind faith. In general terms, leadership implies a following whose behaviour is the result of conscious consideration of the leader's personality, of its own interest and the anticipated social consequences.

Barnabad (1958) in the study of the characteristics of lay leaders in catenation work also indicates that leaders as compared to non-leaders had high social status, owned more land and are better educated. Reports of the diffusion studies done in India clearly show that the leaders had high caste status, higher level of living, greater political awareness of the national scene and were, on the whole, more progressive than non-leaders. Here the another makes a distinction between the two types of leaders in rural India : Community leaders and Opinion leaders. Opinion leaders are informal leaders who are active in the flow of interpersonal influence by disseminating agricultural information where as community leaders are accredited spokesmen for the community who, in consultation with the extension agency, organise and supervise development projects in the local community. Farm size, extension agency contact, news paper exposure, social participation, secular orientation and empathy explain 25 percent of the variance in the community leadership on the other hand, age, farm size, social participation and innovativeness are most significant correlatives of agricultural opinion leadership.

The opinion leaders tend to be older in age and traditional oriented while community leaders tend to be younger progressive in their technological orientation but conventional in their value orientation; they are rational in their self-orientation but traditional in their religious orientation. Community leaders are not rational and liberal but they are also more collectivity oriented than opinion leaders.

LEADERSHIP TRAITS

The grass-root level political system is still, by and large, under the control of leadership which comes from the larger families, and from those who are economically well to do and have a good record of social service to their credit. No doubt, there is a slight break- through in the leadership status in the post-Panchayati Raj era as far as the above factors are concerned, but the whole of economically better off people continues on the mechanism of power as it operates at the village level in all fields of life. Age as a factor of dominance of traditional leadership is losing its importance. With regard to the caste superiority, it was certainly important during the pre-Panchayati Raj period of rural Govt. system. But there is a considerable reverse trend of it in the sense that caste is losing its significance in the present day Panchayat. This does not, however, mean that the lower caste people have started in bulk dominating the political scene at the village level. The representation of lower caste people in Panchayati Raj is there more because of reservation of seats for them. In addition to reservation of seats, the integrative role of the parties, interest groups and secular activities of castes themselves have also brought about a significant change in the dominance of the caste system. "It can be said that the introduction of PRIS. has given rise to a basic change in the socio-economic values of rural society, social change and economic development can be taken as the main responsibility of the emerging leadership at the grass-root level."[4] (Panchayati Raj will literally throw up a new kind of leadership whose value orientations and cultural back ground are essentially, if not entirely, different from those of the elite-leadership which is mainly urban based and west oriented.[5]

Panchayati Raj today presents an "upside-down" image. At the base of the Pyramid appears the nearly 80 percent population of rural India still living in a primitive, pre-scientific and non-industrial age and holding fast to obsolete cultural and social norms and one can clearly mark the counter pressures being generated from this massive and extensive base in response to the change process launched from a narrow apex by an "Active Minority" of elite leaders who have imbibed the cultural values of the modern technological age. The two forces moving in opposite directions are likely to give rise to a variety of collisions and conflicts and with the introduction of Panchayati Raj the number and frequency of such cultural classes" are likely to increase as for the first time, the base- people get a chance to acquire "leadership status" and confront the national elite, particularly the state leaders from a position of considerable bargaining power.

Due to socio-cultural foundations the emerging Panchayati Raj leadership will have to undergo a process of "Re socialization" before it can readily be counted upon to carry forward the "nation building" activities of economic mobilization and socio-political reorganisation.

What is really the emerging trend of leadership at Panchayat level after the first election under the constitutional provisions and also in pursuance of the provisions of the Bihar Panchayati Raj Act, 1993 is being manifested from the following tables dealing with leadership bio-data in one sub-division of Naugachia (Bhagalpur).

Table 1 : Showing Mal-Female Ratio

SEX	NUMBER	PERCENTAGE
Male	63	64.95
Female	34	35.00
Total	97	100.00%

The male-female ratio as indicated in the table is an unusual phenomenon in so far as women have come to share powers at even Panchayat level quite in strength (in our situation 35% of the total respondents.

Prior to the enactment of the latest legislation in Bihar, Panchayat was hardly having an elected women member except those co-opted under the obligation of the previous Panchayat Acts of the State. With provisions made in the 1993 Act the State has also made a provision of reservation of 33 percent seats for women from each social group. This has helped women to reach to the power centre even when we are having male dominated social syndrome.

Table 2: Showing caste composition of members of Panchayats

CATEGORIES	NUMBER	PERCENTAGE
General	17	17.52
O.B.Cs.	66	68.04
S.Cs.	12	12.37
Muslims	2	2.07
Total	97	100.00%

Conventionally, prior to the last elections we had leadership at Panchayat level mostly drawn from upper castes (now under the general category) who also used to weld economic and political powers in their own right. The rural rich had fully utilised the opportunity for controlling the Panchayats either directly or indirectly. By virtue of their elected positions also it was easy for them to preserve and expand their economic control over the entire rural populace in their jurisdiction.

The rural population, not with standing its numerical strength rarely succeeded in occupying elective positions. Never did an exploiting class voluntarily renounce its powers and its capacity to foster their own interests. This way Panchayat system in its previous avtar helped powerful rural classes and linked them to the ruling class of India. The old zamindars saw in the statutory Panchayat system a prospect of compensation for the zamindari they had lost. The outcome of the last Panchayat elections in Bihar has however, turned the table turtile. Now those upper castes falling in General category is contended with merely 17.52 percent seats while O.B.Cs. are massively there in the position of power, they being 68.04 of the total population. It is not that their growing strength is due to reservation for them- they have increased their strength by utilising number card besides the additional privilege of being under the reserved category. Those in general category have now to be reconciled in view of their shrinking numerical strength vis-a-vis the O.B.Cs.

Though people belonging to scheduled castes are besides having state protections by way of reservation both in elected position and also education and employment however, they have not emerged so vigorously as is the case with the O.B.Cs. The O.B.Sc. are presently there to share the cake massively.

Table 3: Showing Age distribution of Leaders

AGE GROUP	NUMBER	PERCENTAGE
18-32 years	36	37.11
33-45 years	41	42.26
46-60 years	18	18.56
60 & above	2	2.07
Total	97	100.00%

The table shows that those belonging to 18-32 years and also middle aged have occupied the leadership position more than those elders belonging to 46-60 years and 60 and above years. The emerging situation very much suggests that Panchayats now attract both young and middle aged persons which is a contrast to the previous trend in   Panchayat elections when elderly people had their advantage to be in the position of powers even though they had lost their vigour to exert for the welbing of the people particularly, the weaker sections.

Things appear to have now turned to be different. The younger people are now in the seats of powers and are expected to do things more vigorously than their counterparts did in the past.

Table 4: Showing educational level of Panchayat leadership

LEVEL OF EDUCATION	NUMBER	PERCENTAGE
Illiterate	12	12.37
Primary	34	35.05
Secondary	40	41.24
Graduate	8	8.25
Graduation and above	3	3.09

Education play an important role in articulating opinions and moulding the aspirations. It is a happy sign that people with different educational background have turned to participate in Panchayat activities. This really officers bureaucrats and baboos attached to Panchayati system. As the story goes the previous leadership felt shy while dealing with the Govt. functionaries because of their inferior educational background. The situation ought to be now some what different.

Table 5: Showing Occupational Status of Panchayat leaders

OCCUPATION	NUMBER	PERCENTAGE
Service	2	2.07
Agriculture	6	6.18
Private job	39	40.21
Others	50	51.54
Total	97	100.00

Prior to the last Panchayat elections in Bihar Panchayat used to be the domain of landlords and agriculturists as they were the people of dominate both economically and socially. Situation has since drastically changed. For securing a position in power structure economic status of the aspirant does hardly count. Any person with his/her personal ambition can try for an elective position which does not demand his/her economic affluence or so.

Table 6: Showing the landowning Status of the Leaders

LAND HOLDING	NUMBER	PERCENTAGE
Landless	10	10.30
Marginal Farmer (Less than 2.5 acres)	67	69.07
Small Farmers (2.5 to 5 acres)	18	18.56
Above 5 Acres	2	2.07

The table suggests that economically lowlier people are more in the leadership rank at Panchayat level than those from relatively well-off sections. There was a time when only landlords and money-lenders took Panchayat leadership as their preserve as aginst this now it is the turn of marginal farmers and landless population to share power at Panchayat level. Thank to the emerging trend of social transformation. The traditional leadership generally constituted of landlords, rich peasants and traders, who usually belonged to upper caste families. By securing legitimate powers they could preserve and expand their economic control over the rural population. The rural poor, not withstanding its numerical strength, hardly succcccded in occupying elective positions. In fact, Panchayats institution sub-observed their interests. They had heavy stake in maintaining socio-economic status quo. They were not so much sympathetic to the weaker sections of the village whose prosperity, they believed, would be at their own expense. Last but not the least for decades Panchayat remained captive of insensitive, selfish, arrogant, undemocratic and also exploitative leaders leaving no scope for the institution to justify their existence as an instrument of economic development and social change.

Table 7: Showing Income Status of Leaders at Panchayat level

INCOME GROUP	NUMBER	PERCENTAGE
Rs. 1500 per month	40	41.24
Rs. 3000 per month	38	39.17
Rs. 6000 per month	14	14.44
Rs. 6000 and above	5	5.15

The table discussing Income status of leaders at Panchayat level also corroborates the fact that economic criteria had in no sense any relevance for joining the rank of leadership. Instead, what we have seen is that the poorer have come to share more the cake of power than those better off. This gives us the hope that bereft of caste and class, the two determining factors for leadership in yore years, the present leadership is expected to serve the interest of the preponderant weaker people more than what was done for them by the previous set up of leadership. Active as well as mature section of the population have come to take initiative. A good number of leaders are educated persons. If they put their heart and soul together in refurbishing the fading Panchayat system they can very much do it in view of their numerical strength. So far the emphasis has been to shift from community beneficiary to individual beneficiary. The present set up of leadership has the potentiality to stop all the 'monkey business' that went unhindered in the past. It is expected to instill in the people a sense of partnership in development programmes and seek their cooperation and support in their implementation. Further more, by effective planning and implementation it can utilise the available resources by taking into account local interests. The present day rural leadership can very much help mobilise local resources in the delivery of inputs and services. The leadership can communicate the requirements of the people in voicing their concern at higher rungs of administration. This sort of communication and interaction would positively facilitate in strengthening the administrative accountability and responsiveness in the sphere of socio-economic development.

NOTES AND REFERENCES

1.   Donglas Esminger quoted by S.B. Batnagar "The Nehru Model of Nation Building" published in Democracy, Pluralism and Nation Building (ed) 1984- p. 60, NBO. Publishers and Distributors.

2.   Govt. of India (1961) pp. 338-39.

3.   Y. Bhakar Rao- Emerging Leadership Among S.Cs/S.Ts. under New Panchayat Raj Act in Karnatak (2001), p. 5- NIRI).

4.   Y. Bhaskar Rao- Op.Cit. p. 10.

5.   P.C. Mathur- Op.Cit. p. 128.

EXTENT OF EMPOWERMENT OF PANCHAYATS UNDER THE PROVISIONS OF THE BIHAR PANCHAYAT RAJ ACT, 1993

Panchayats have been grappling with problems of their existence right their inception after India became independent. There were a few states only where the Panchayats got the state patronage and were pushed off by state powers to any extent. In majority of states they were almost stemmed and immeasurably constrained to take off. Reviewing their performance Ashok Mehta Committee (1978) had remarked : "corruption, inefficiency, scant regard for procedures, political interference in day to day administration, motivated actions, power concentration, all these have seriously limited the utility of Panchayati Raj for the average villagers." The committee further stated that except in Maharastra and Gujrat the Panchayati Raj institutions have rarely been given opportunity to take up planning and implementation on any worth while scale. Activities of Panchayati Raj institutions were megre, their resource base weak and overall attention given to them niggardly." The G.V.K. Rao Committee in 1985 and M. Singvi Committee in 1986 were also very unhappy over the prevailing affairs in the Panchayati system.

The Rao Committee Report observed that the PRIS. were sabotaged by bureaucracy and vested interests in most places. "They had acted in connivance with legislators and M.Ps. from the respective areas under the impression that Panchayati Raj is a still born scheme commented L.M. Singhvi. For Rajni Kothari (1993) Panchayati Raj itself being reduced to gimmick.

Recalling to the days of Community Development project initiated in early fifties when Panchayat was also proposed to act as an agent of economic development and social change we have evidences when Panchayats as a system was deliberately ignored and not allowed to grow to the extent of assuming its responsibility as an agent of economic development and social change. Panchayats which was supposed to be a unit of Govt. at the village level as recommended in the Second Five Year Plan could not grow on the desired lines. Hugh Tinker's observation that in general Panchayat experiment has shown the same discouraging refusal to "get off the ground" as before, has ample justification. Adia Doctor had observed " Panchayats have done very little with their statutory powers- that even when they are formally responsible for preparing plans ..." it is the officials who did the job and most of the Panchayats restricted their activities to municipal function like street lighting, water supply. In general village Panchayats seldom meet and whey they do it- it is socially to conduct regular business such as "selecting office bearers and thelike."[1]

About the role played by the village Panchayats in the development administration the study Team on Plan Project, also known as Balwant Rai Committee (1957) observed : "The available information indicates that possibly not more than 10% of the total number of a Panchayat are functioning effectively, roughly, one half are average and the remaining 40% are working unsatisfactorily ... The actual performance of Panchayats is generally limited to making arrangements for sanitation, conservancy, construction and repair of fair weather roads, provision of domestic water supply and street lighting. Even these simple and elementary civic functions are not being performed with a degree of efficiency over large areas- only small number of Panchayats those situated within or near the block areas have shown a zeal for development activities on any appreciable scale.[2]

Explaining financial crisis facing Panchayats the Balwant Rai Mehta study Team observed : The Panchayats are generally handicapped for want of adequate financial resources to meet the growing expenditures on local programmes of development. It is evident that without financial assistance from the State Govt. many Panchayats cannot continue their existence. It would appear from the available data that the majority of working Panchayats over large areas have annual income not exceeding   Rs. 500/- from all sources including Govt. subsidy. Deducting the cost of small establishments maintained by the Panchayats, on account of pay of the Secretary who is whole time or part time in many cases, conservancy staff, contingencies and contribution for the up keep of Nyay Panchayats, very little is left for construction and welfare activities. There are three major aspects of the problem relating to finance : inadequate resources allotted to Panchayats under the Acts, a general reluctance among Panchayats to make use of the existing resources and general inefficiency in tax administration. In the sphere of finance, some of the difficulties are partly administrative and even temperamental. Not all Panchayats levy even compulsory taxes and fewer collect them with any degree of efficiency. In Bihar, Orissa and Madhya Pradesh, it is reliably learnt that the collection don't exceed 25-30%. In many cases sarpanchas and Panchas are among the defaulters. The complaints of discriminations in assessment are fairly common and in a few cases a deliberative victimization. The assessment lists are not periodically revised. There is a general aversion to adopt coercive measures, which, it is feared, will make the Panchayats unpopular. It is well to bear in mind that the general failure to assess and collect the various taxes and fees has wider repercussions. It creates an atmosphere unfavourable to the growth of the Panchayats."[3]

Keeping in view all those constraints which marred Panchayats to grow in their own right the Balwant Rai Mehta Committee Report had recommended, "The team was of definite view that the time had arrived in India when central and State Govts. must repose greater faith and trust the people for their own welfare. They also suggested that basic unit of local Govt., for purposes of development should be the village Panchayat. Maximum of power should be devolved and delegated to this body for implementation of community development programme which falls within the territorial jurisdiction of the village.[4]

The National Development Committee (NDC) accepted the basic recommendations of the study Team in 1958. The Third Five Yearn Plan brought out the primary object of Panchayati Raj in these words : "The Primary objectives of Panchayati Raj is to enable the people of each area to achieve intensive and continuous development in the interest of the entire population ... It comprehend both the democratic institutions and extension services through which development programmes are executed.

Concept of Panchayati Raj was also discussed during the seminar on Fundamental Problems of Panchayati Raj held in January, 1964 at Banglore under the auspicious of the All India Panchayat Parishad and accordingly PRIS are the units of Govt. at their respective level. Power belongs to the people. Instead of a centre parceling out power to the states the Zila Parishad so on down below, it is the people down below who will give over residual powers to the upper levels. No longer the apex of the social pyramid for its own strengthening or for its well being decide as to where how much power should reside. It is the base that will take these decisions. Finally it came out of the seminar that the objectives of the Panchayati Raj is to generate in local people the capacity to take initiative in dealing with problems of economic and social development. The real purpose is to awaken rural India and generate a feeling of confidence and self reliance and utilizing latent energy and potentialities, a decentralized apparatus with necessary help from the Govt. and technical people had to be arranged." S.K. Dey, a great advocate of Panchayati Raj and cooperative Movement and also a Union Minister had observed : "In India Panchayati Raj is the name of the present system of local self Governing Institutions, most of which were established after 1959. In its objectives as well as in its scope and content, Panchayati Raj is different from any reform of local Govt. attempted in the past and is an administrative revolution with immense potentialities for future advance. It seeks to effect a fundamental change in the centralised bureaucratic administrative apparatus that had been established in India by the U.K. and remained in effect after India had attained independence."[5] Giving reasons for adoption of Panchayati Raj as a system of administration S.R. Nanekar stated : "Two consideration seems to have accelerated the process of democratic decentralisation in India. In the first place, the will to strengthen the base of democracy itself has dictated the adoption of measures for establishing effective popular local units of Govt. at various levels in the Indian states, namely, the Zila, the Block and the Village. And second the realisation of the need for popular local Govt. for propagating the ideas of our plans and securing people's cooperation in their execution."[6]

The historic Congress Session at Bhavanagar in early 1961 gave a mandate to all states to speed up legislation and implement the programmes of democratic decentralisation. The Govt. of India also laid the following basic guidelines for Panchayati Raj.[7]

1. It should be a three tier structure of local self governing bodies from the village to the district- the body being organically linked.

2. There should be a genuine transfer of power and responsibility to them.

3. Adequate resources should be transferred to the new bodies to enable them to discharge these responsibilities.

4. All developmental programmes at these levels should be channeled through these bodies.

5. The system evolved should be such as will facilitate further devolution and dispersal of power and responsibilities in the future.

Village Panchayats which had fallen into desuetude were, in the changing situation expected to exercise heavy responsibilities in the backdrops of so many serious thoughts given for its revival as an agency of economic growth and social changes. Under the new scheme of Panchayati Raj Panchayats were to be the nucleolus of Planning and Instrument for execution of schemes of rural development. Panchayat was to be the edifice on which the entire organisational structure of Panchayati Raj as a whole would stand. Conceptually Panchayat as an institution was an extension of the Parliamentary system of Govt. buttressed by an element of direct democracy.

Now the point is how these loud talks and national policies for the proper functioning of Panchayats after Indian Independence could help the institution to grow so as to resume its lost status besides becoming an effective agent for economic development and social change particularly in rural areas. In this connection it is relevant for us to take Bihar as a case. Prior to the 73rd constitutional amendment there were various state enactments in Bihar governing Panchayati Raj scheme of administration. The last important enactment was the Bihar Panchayat Samitis and Zila Parishads Act, 1961. It was this 1961 enactment which virtually sought for the effective transfer of powers to Panchayati Raj bodies under the spirit of decentralisation.

However when provisions of the 1961 Act are analysed it is evidently proved that various restrictions imposed on these institutions within the framework of the Acthardly paved way for any amount of decentralisation not to talk of allowing village Panchayats to assume the role of a democratic institution caring for economic development and social change. Empirical researches[8] have more or less common conclusion that the "Govt. have failed to realise the perceptive of the control and instead of assuming the role of helper friend and guide the Govt. is acting in the old fashion of looking to them as its agents. To cit a few : state control over Panchayati Raj bodies was felt necessary only to the extent it was positive, constructive and stimulating but to the contrary it is negative, inquisitorial and stifling. Ignoring certain basic qualities inherent in the system the Govt. has considerably increased its power of control over them as if these institutions can not be judicious to the obligations thrushed on them. Moreover, the provisions of the Act do not allow determination of the will of the people. So much so that we have seen even in minor matters of appointment and dismissal PRIS. have to depend on the approval of the State Govt. Govt. Sanction has to be invariably obtained in the matter of execution of scheme irrespective of the amount of scheme which ultimately cause unnecessary delay telling upon the efficiency of the PRIS. The delicacies faced by the PRIS. reflect in themselves that element of distrust determines the relationship between the State Govt and PRIS. such a situation is quite contradictory to the picture drawn by the Committee on plan project which had envisaged that "if this body is to function with any vigour, initiative and success, the Govt. will have to devolve upon it all its functions in the fields of development within the body's jurisdiction reserving to itself the function of guidance, supervision and higher planning and where necessary providing for extra funds" (Sec. 28, Vol. I of the Report). But as against this there seems to be decentralised administration through centralised directives. Instead of becoming Govt. at their own level as envisaged initially, Panchayati Raj institutions have to work as limbs of the State Govt." Corroborating such findings about the actual status of PRIS. S.R. Nanekar also observed : "the tendency on the part of the State Govt. has naturally been to retain maximum possible control over the local Govts. Added to this the financial powers of the State Govt. over the local Govts. and the list of powers becomes formidable enough to enable the former to brow beat the latter into any submissive action.[9]

"In the matter of funds also, Panchayati Raj bodies have come to rely solely on Govt. grants. These grants are tied to specific projects and Grant receiving agencies have to act as agencies to Grants sanctioning authorities. Acting as the agencies of the Govt. Panchayati Raj bodes have to fulfill series of official obligations in the matter of its expenditure. The Grant giving authorities acquire the right to issue directions from time to time during the execution of the schemes for which Grants have been received."[10] This had resulted in progressive loss of interest in planning and development on the part of Panchayat leadership who being deprived of any scope of initiative remain engaged in petty administrative matters.

Viewed from all the states facts it is safe to conclude that in the Panchayati Raj system under the Bihar Panchayat Samitis and Zila Parishads Act, 1961 power had been delegated instead of devolving to them. They were nothing more than glorified state agencies. It was an unhappy mixture of devolution Governmental interference stood in the way of freedom of action. "The two great enemies of realistic planning for rural development- order coming from head quarters and imposed assignments without taking into consideration local conditions are still dominating the scene. Programmes of Panchayati Raj bodies are also drawn up and targets fixed by the Govt. The gulf between paper achievements and actualities is still widening. It seems, the spirit of democratic decentralisation has, if at all it has, touched the fringe and not the core of state administration. In the name of Panchayati Raj a 'hybrid system' of administration has emerged."[11] Quoting Chetakar Jha in this regard : one cannot help feeling that the entire system is based on suspicion about the capacity, ability and impartiality of the leaders at the local kid to manage local affairs. Truth of the matter is that it is not a system of decentralisation at all. The title of the scheme is perhaps in the nature of proper noun' the meaning of which need not indicate the traits and qualities of the person bearing a particular name. Decentralisation is a political concept."[12]

We can thus evidently state that in Bihar PRIS. were hardly given the scope to act up to themselves. The scheme remained sandwiched between political leaders and bureaucrat nexus. The amount of restraints imposed on the functioning of these institutions under the State Act coupled with callousness of the bureaucracy apparently throttled PRIS. in its very infancy.

Now let us examine the extent of empowerment to the Panchayats under the provisions of the Bihar Panchayati Raj Act, 1993 obviously enacted under the obligations of the 73rd amendment of the Indian constitution which basically seeks to bring both democracy and devolution of powers to Panchayats. Panchayats have now become part of the constitution of the country. No one can snatch democratic practices from Panchayats. Panchayats can't now be kept arbitrarily suspended or dissolved. No one will be able to take away the powers, responsibilities and finances devolved upon the Panchayats. The State Act of 1993, obviously, while enacting the law empowering Panchayats must have been inspired by the very spirit of the amendment provisions.

The Bihar Panchayati Raj Act, 1993 has allocated following functions to a Panchayat.

Function of Village Panchayat :

I.   General functions :

1.   To formulate annual plans for the development of areas falling within the Panchayat jurisdiction;

2.   To prepare annual budget;

3.   Power to ensure Relief and rehabilitation to the people affected during natural calamities;

4.   To remove encroachments from public prosperity;

5.   To organise shramdan for community works;

6.   To maintain village statistics.

II.   Agriculture including Agriculture extension :

1.   Development and improvement of agriculture and horticulture in Panchayat areas;

2.   Development of waste land;

3.   Development and maintenance of grazing lands and restraining its illegal transfer and use.

III.   **Animal husbandry, Dairy and Paltry farm :**

1.   Improvement of animal and paltry breed;

2.   Extension of cattle enclosure, paltry farm and piggery.

3.   Development of dairy farm.

IV.   **Encouragement for Fisheries within Panchayat areas.**

V.   **Social Forestry, Minor Forest Produce, Small area forest, fuel and fodder.**

1.   Encouragement for plantation of trees on public land in Panchayat areas and also their maintenance.

2.   Encouragement for plantation of trees for fuel purposes and also cultivation of fodder.

3.   Encouragement for forest based industries.

4.   Encouragement for social forestry.

VI.   **Promotion of village and cottage industries.**

1.   To promote awareness among the village population for their common benefit organise workshop, seminar, training programmes also demonstration of agricultural and industrial activities going around in Panchayat areas.

VII.   **Village Housing Scheme :**

1.   Distribution of housing sits;

2.   Preserving records of house sites and also other private and public properties.

VIII.   **Drinking water:**

1.   Construction, repair and maintenance of tube wells, wells and tank.

2.   Prevention and control of spread of water pollution;

3.   Construction and maintenance of village drinking water projects;

IX.   **Road, Building, culverts, setu etc. :**

1.   Construction and maintenance of village Roads, drainage and culverts;

2.   Maintenance of Govt. Buildings and also those masons donated to a Panchayat by the public or a person.

3.   Boat service and its maintenance.

X.   **Rural electrification to ensure that light is available in public places including village lanes.**

XI.   **Promotion of non-conventional sources of Energy.**

    1.   Popularising bio-gas scheme and also improved over project for rural.

XII.   **Poverty alleviation projects :**

1. Creating job opportunities for the Panchayat population and also publicity for job opportunities under the schemes of self employment among them.

2. Identification of persons to be covered under the Below Poverty Line through Gram Sabha.

3. To extend cooperation to the agencies engaged in the execution of poverty alleviation schemes and also their monitoring.

XIII.   **Education – Primary and Middle :**

1. To promote and awareness among the illiterate rural population about the advantages of education.

2. To ensure large scale admissions and also full and regular attendance of students studying in such schools.

XIV.   **Encouraging the system of adult education.**

1. To promote adult education among the illiterate population of the Panchayat.

XV.   **Cultural Activities :**

1. Promotion of social and cultural activities.

XVI.   **Market and Fair**

1. Organising fair including of cables on the eve of public festivals.

XVIII **Village Sanitation :**

1. To ensure general sanitation inside villages

2. Cleaning of public plans like Road, drain, pond, well and other places of common use.

3. Provision of burial sites (for both Hindus and Muslims) and their proper maintenance.

4. Construction and maintenance of public laboratories.

5. Disposal of disowned dead bodies and carcasses.

6. Provision and maintenance of bathing and washing ghats in village ponds.

IXX   **Public Health and Welfare :**

1. Execution of welfare schemes and monitoring functioning of health centres.

2. Eradication of epidemics and also ensuring proper treatment to the victims of the epidemics.

3. Ensuring marketisation of meat, fish and other perishable eating materials.

4.   To extend cooperation to functionaries engaged in vaccination jobs against diseases for both men and cattle.

5.   To issue license for starting entertainment shows and also for hotels and stalls in public land falling in Panchayat jurisdiction.

6.   Disposal of the dead street dogs.

7.   Regulating the business of skins and leather in Panchayat areas.

8.   Regulating objectionable and dangerous avocations.

XX.   Women and Child Welfare :

1.   To extend cooperation in the schemes meant for women and child welfare.

2.   Supervision and inspection of schools, health centres and also schemes of Nutrition for the children.

XXI.   Social Welfare including the welfare of physically handicapped and mentally retarded persons.

1.   To extend cooperation in execution of social welfare schemes aiming at the welfare of physically handicapped, mentally retarded and also for those who need outside help.

2.   To monitor and supervise distribution of money as old age and widow pension.

XXII.   Welfare of weaker sections of society particularly schedule castes and scheduled tribes population

1.   To promote public awareness about the measures being taken for the welfare of weaker sections of the society particularly the schedule castes and scheduled tribes.

2.   To extend cooperation in the execution of schemes seeking welfare of the weaker sections including scheduled castes and tribes.

XXIII.   Public Distribution System :

1.   To promote people's awareness about the essential commodities being supplied through public distribution system.

2.   To monitor the distribution system.

XXIV.   Maintenance and control of Community Assets :

1.   To maintain community Assets.

2.   Locating Community Assets and maintenance thereof.

XXV.   Construction and maintenance of rest houses and other institution of public utility.

XXVI.   Construction and maintenance of Khatals, Thela stands and Kazi house.

XXVII.   Construction and maintenance of slaughter house.

XXVIII.   Maintenance of public park, playing grounds etc.

XXIX.   Location of garbage sites in public grounds.

XXX.   Construction of hutments and their maintenance.

XXXI.   Such other jobs to be entrusted to a Panchayat by the State Govt. from time to time.

These are the latest provision for empowerment to Panchayat in its new avtar.

Now the point is- in actuality how do things stand when viewed empirically?

As a matter of fact, efforts have been made by the State Govt. to transfer all those responsibilities to Panchayat departmental wise. If taken together 21 departments of the State Govt. have so far issued directions to the district collectors and other subordinate officers to give effct to the transfer of responsibilities to PRIS. including Panchayats.[13] These departments are Agriculture, Revenue and Land Reform Minor Irrigation, Animal Husbandry and Fisheries, Environment and forest, Industry, Public Health engineering, Rural Development, Energy, Primary education, Adult education, Secondary education, Arts, culture and youth, Health-Medical Education and Family welfare, welfare, social welfare, Labour-Employment and Training, Food-supply and commerce, Relief and Rehabilitation.

There is no gainsaying that the constitution mandate in 73rd Amendment envisaging empowerment of Panchayats with financial and administrative responsibilities has opened a new vista for good governance. However, at the same time, one can clearly observe that Panchayats still suffer from the dependency syndrome and grass roots democracy envisaged through Panchayats in the true sense remains a far cry.

The British legacy of distrust by the people placed higher in states and rank of those placed below in the hierarchy is still persists. The distrust has enmeshed grass-roots democratic structures as well. This has in turn resulted in indifferent and fragmented functioning among Panchayat and village level workers.

The second significant feature of the village scenario is the under utilisation of the available infrastructure e.g. Panchayat ghar, school, Angnabari centre and others.

Thirdly, the Govt. field functionaries responsible for delivery of services at village/ Panchayat level work in a disparate and segmented manner with a narrow departmental approach. Each worker looks at problems and implements the assigned scheme in a compartmentalized manner a their sectors in hierarchy never take a holistic and integrated view.

Lack of awareness about Govt's. policies, programmes and schemes is another significant feature of our rural scene. T.V. Channel and Radio network among themselves have almost covered the entire country but most of the programmes leave much to be desired in terms of educating and orienting the rural citizenry for seeking feed back and response to Govt. policies and programmes. Even Programmes dedicated to agriculture like Krishi Jagat or Chaupal air routinised information and, at times, outdated knowledge about techniques and methods of farming and improvement of rural life. Lack of awareness among rural folk has not only resulted into in difference towards Govt's. policies, programmes and schemes but has, on the contrary, diverted to attractive populist channels and programmes like film shows and serials.[14]

NOTES & REFERENCES

1. Adih Doctor-studies in Indian Democracies (1965) p. 375- Allied Publisher.

2. Section 3, Vol. I of the Report of the study Team of committee on Plan Project (1957) Committee on Plan Project.

3. Sec. 2.3, Vol. I of the Report of the study Team of committee on Plan Project.

4. Op. Cit., Sec. 3, Vol. I.

5. S.K. Dey – Kurukshetra – 28th Jan. 1962, P. 17.

6. S.R. Nanekar- Dilemma of Democratic Politics in India (1961) P. 104 – Manak Tulas.

7. Panchayati Raj at a Glance (1966) Govt. of India Publications.

8. G.N. Thakur – unpublished Theses on "working of Panchay at Semitis and Zila Parishads in Bihar's (1975) Bihar University.

9. S.R. Nanekar – Op. Cit. 107.

10. G.N. Thakur – Op. Cit. P. 248.

11. G.N. Thakur – Op. Cit. p. 252.

12. Chetakar Jha – His paper on "Circumstances of Leadership" Presented in a seminar.

13. Panchayati Raj Directorate – Rural Development Department – Oct. 2001.

14. L.C. Srivastav "Empowering Panchayats for good Governance" Yojna – Oct. 2000, pp. 29-31.

FINANCIAL AUTONOMY GRANTED TO PANCHAYATS UNDER THE ACT

Finance is a pervasive aspect of administrative operation. No system of governance can run successfully unless there is a provision for adequate finance for consolidation and reorganisation of local governing institutions not merely requires efficient structure but also sufficient finance to discharge their duties effectively. It is because of the significant role of finance in the working of any institution of autonomous nature that there is a budgetary system. This will be evident when we go through the kind of deliberations about strengthening Panchayats as local government institution even in the long past.

The Royal Commission of Decentralisation had considered as early as in 1907-08 that Panchayats should get a portion of the landless levied for the local board purposes in the village, they should get special grants for particular objects of local importance, receipt from village cattle ponds and markets entrusted to their management and small fees on civil suits filed before them.

The Local Finance Enquiry Committee (1951) had suggested to restore to Panchayats following item of taxes.[1]

1.   Taxes on land and buildings

2.   Taxes on entry of goods into local areas for consumption, use or sale therein.

3.   Taxes on advertisements other than advertisements published in News Papers.

4.   Taxes on vehicles other than those mechanically propelled.

5.   Taxes on animals and boats

6.   Taxes on profession, trades, callings and employment.

Considering deplorable financial conditions of most of the Panchayats, the Local Finance Enquiry Committee felt that financial assistance also from other sources to Panchayats was necessary and thus they recommended for an unconditional allotment of the 15% of land revenue to village Panchayats raised in the Panchayats area. In addition, there should be a surcharge on the transfer of immovable property within the Panchayats jurisdiction, the proceeds of which should go to Panchayats funds. Further, village should be assisted by the State Govt. in the following manners :

i.   Salaries and allowances of Panchayats officers should be borne by the State Govt. at least to the extent of 3/4th.

ii.   Wherever Panchayats are essentially required to maintain Chowkidars and Daffadars for watch and ward duties, the State Govt. should bear the cost on account of their salaries and allowances.

iii.   Panchayats should be allowed the use of State Govt. lands within their jurisdiction.

iv.   Village Panchayats, where ever possible, should be encouraged to collect land revenue and landless on behalf of the State Govt. on a Commission basis.

v.   Panchayats should also be encouraged to undertake as many remunerative enterprises as possible, namely markets, slaughter houses, cart and bus stands and ferries.

vi.   Panchayats should also be encouraged to take up cooperative farming, dairies and such like activities under the guidance of the State Govt.

There have been various suggestions and recommendations, for argumentation of Panchayats' financial resources from time to time. A reference to such recommendations by the study Team on Panchayati Raj Finance (1963) after the introduction of Panchayati Raj based on Balwant Rai Mehta team's recommendations needs to be mentioned here.

The measures suggested by the study Team on Panchayati Raj Finance[2] can be divided into two parts- the first part relates to strengthening of personal funds and the second part concerns to governmental assistance. For strengthening personal funds following measures were suggested :

Taxation: The Study Team had recommended two types of taxes- compulsory and supplementary. Under Compulsory taxes comes (a) House, (b) Profession, and (c) Vehicles.

Supplementary Taxes: Panchayats, according to the recommendations of the study team should be given comprehensive powers to :

(a)   License fee for registrations of cattle brought for sale, collection of hides and skins, Tea stalls and restaurants, goods exposed in the market, for direction of new buildings, for use of common lands and community property and for carrying on offensive or dangerous trades;

(b)   to impose fines and penalties for encroachments, failure to take license and unauthorized possession of or dealing in prohibited articles;

(c)   Where water supply, electric lighting or drainage supply is provided through loans a Panchayat should charge a fee from each beneficiary.

Special Taxes: The study Team had also recommended that Panchayats should have the power to levy special taxes based on land revenue, house tax or on some other items for executing specific development projects. It should be valid for one year but maybe renewed by a resolutions.

Assets to be transferred:

i)   Since village Panchayats are the integral part of the State Govt. the study Team had suggested for vesting all properties of the State Govt. at the village level which can be managed by Panchayats.

ii)   Unless specifically exempted following properties situated in a Panchayat area and not belonging to a private party should be transferred to the Panchayats :

    (a)   all lands

    (b)   all trees

    (c)   Ponds, tanks and fishery right therein

    (d)   unreserved forest

    (e)   Rest house and other buildings.

iii)   Out of cultivable land which have not been assigned to individuals for cultivation, a minimum of 1 percent of land per capita should be given to each Panchayat to be utilised as non-alienable community property. At the same time, wherever necessary State Govt. should acquire not less than 5 acres of land and hand over to each Panchayats to be used as community property for house sites, compost making, tree planting and for such other purposes,

iv)   Wherever fishing right customarily belongs to local communities of fishermen, the management of the pond or tank should vest in Panchayats.

STATE ASSISTANCE

In regard to state assistance to Panchayats the study Team on Panchayati Raj Finance had recommended following categories of State Govt. assistance to Panchayats :

1.   Stamp duty, according to the study Team, was eminently suitable for strengthening the finances of Panchayats. It is the purchaser or mortgager of the property that pays the duty, it does not affect the general population.

2.   Another important tax, the proceeds of which maybe given wholly or party to Panchayats, is the State Entertainment Tax. Panchayats may levy a show Tax is addition.

3.   The assistance in the part or whole salary of the Secretary of Panchayats should be in the form of purposive Grant (It was felt essential for Panchayats to make payments of salary to its Secretary directly).

4.   In order to induce Panchayats to raise the rates above the minimum and encourage prompt and regular collection, the Study Team had recommended that on the entire tax demand of a Panchayat MATCHING GRANT should be given to Panchayats doing their jobs effectively.

5.   In order to bring psychological revolution in Panchayats the Study Team had recommended for an assistance of Rs. 1/- per capita from the Central and State Govts. By doing so, the Team felt, Panchayats will be able to raise more than they do at present from their own resources and exploit fully the compulsory and optional taxes.

LOANS

Panchayats according to the recommendation of the Study Team may build up their funds from loans also. But money should be borrowed for undertaking remunerative enterprises only such as construction of shops, markets, hotels, cinema house, purchase of tractors, agricultural implements and other requirements to be hire, out to agriculturists and cooperative societies and for plantation and forestation and establishing small scale industries.

To make loans of desired amount available to the Panchayats the Team had recommended for the establishment of Panchayati Raj Finance Cooperation.

These recommendations notwithstanding not even scant regard was ever given by the State power for a follow up of these recommendations. If done so things must have been different today with Panchayats.

Prior to the coming of recommendations of the Study Team on Panchayati Raj Finance (1963) we had already Panchayats working under a separate Act of the Bihar Panchayat Raj Act, 1947. Let us have a look on the provisions made in the Act strengthening financial status of the then Panchayats which were in existence through out the (undivided) State of Bihar?

According to Section 46 of the Act, Revenue of village Panchayats had to be raised from various sources which included in main :

1. Local Taxation : Compulsory (which a Panchayat was obliged to levy) and supplementary (which a Panchayat might or might not levy).

2. Charging fees for services rendered.

3. Profit from community Assets

4. Fines and fees charged by Panchayat Courts.

5. Commission from the State Govt. for collecting land Revenue within Panchayat area.

6. Agency activities of Panchayats in regard to development schemes and profit derived there from.

7. Govt. Grants for General and specific purposes.

TAX

Panchayat had to Levy Tax on property as a part of compulsory Tax in the manner prescribed by the State Govt. Besides, they could also levy taxes on the following sources :

i.   A license fee on persons practicing as professional buyers, brokers, commission agents, weighers or measures

ii.   A tax on persons engaged in any calling (other than agriculture) profession or trade within the jurisdiction of the Panchayat.

iii.   A tax on the vehicle, pack animals and porters bringing goods for sale into the village.

iv.   Fees on goods exposed for sale in any market or place belonging to or under the control of the Panchayat.

v.   Fees on registration of animals sold within the area of the Panchayat.

vi.   Fees for the use of SARAI, Dharmshala, Rest House and encamping grounds vested in the Gram Panchayat.

vii.   A pilgrim tax at place of worship and pilgrimage within the village approved by the State Govt.

Panchayat might also charge special fees for having provided for the benefit of local community certain kinds of services. Special mention had been made about those fees in the Act itself.

i)   Water Tax

ii)   Latrine Tax

iii)   Lighting Tax

iv)   Drainage Tax.

Panchayat subject to an immediate report to the State Govt. or the officer, prescribed in the Act, could impose an Emergency Tax to meet emergent situation arising in Panchayats area.

Assignment of Share of Taxes levied by the State Govt.

Panchayat was allowed under the Act to get an average of 6.25 commission from the State Govt. for collection of Land Revenue on behalf of the State Govt.

Revenue from Non-Taxing Sources :

1.   Until 1959 Labour Tax was of compulsory nature but the system was abandoned and has been replaced by another system of SHARAMDAN (offer of voluntary labour) by the people as envisaged by the Bihar Panchayat Raj (Amendment and validating Act, 1959).

2.   Fines and fees charged by the Panchayat Court also constitutes Panchayat fund.

3.   Some of the agency activities of the Panchayats in regard to the execution of development schemes was also deemed to enhance Panchayat funds.

4. Properties situated within the area of a Panchayat except specifically excluded have been vested in the Panchayats and any income accruing from them was to be treated as the income to Panchayat funds.

5. Panchayats were entitled to build up community assets which besides the existing property and assets might become an additional source of income to them.

6. A Gram Panchayat could enter in to a contract with the Govt. or any local body for the purpose of collecting all or any class of tax payable to the Govt. or to such local body on being allowed a prescribed percentage of collection charges, or to execute any work of embankment or irrigation or any work connected with Rural development schemes or with relief and rehabilitation.

7. All markets or fairs or such portion thereof as are held upon public lands were to be managed and regulated by the Executive Committee and all dues levied or imposed in respect thereof was to be credited to the Panchayat's fund.

8. A Panchayat could also raise funds by resorting to borrowings.

Grants-in-Aids from the Central and State Govts. :

In case of funds collected out of the above mentioned sources still proved inadequate a Gram Panchayat was free to seek grants from the Govt. for purposes to be mentioned in specific terms. Though no definite pattern for Governmental grants was ever laid down however, in principle Panchayats were entitled to seek grants from Govts. when ever they faced financial strain. The State Govt. on its part was committed to aid Panchayats for the following specific purposes :

1. Payment of salary to the staff of the Panchayat

2. 50% of the total cost involved in construction of community hall in Panchayat. The remaining 50% was to be managed by Panchayats themselves.

3. For taking up projects under local works programme the State Govt. was committed to contribute 50 percent of the actual cost involved in the execution of the project.

4. The Govt. of India in order to encourage Panchayats had announced a matching grant to those Panchayats who succeeded in raising at least Rs. 1.77 per capital income of the population residing within Panchayat area through its own resources.

There were so much of scope provided in the Act for augmenting Panchayats' resources is evident from what ever we have discussed about it is previous pages.

Now the basic thing to know is what had been the financial status of the then Panchayats within the frame work of wider scope of raising funds? Unfortunately we have had no empirical data to bring out the truth, however, a study conducted in early seventies on this particular point in the districts of Ranchi and Dhanbad suggested that the average collection of tax out of its own resources hardly came to Rs. 35/- per Panchayat annually in Ranchi district while in all the 21 Panchayats in Dhanbad district, the over all amount collected during the year 1970-71 was merely Rs. 80.41. If we talk of State Govt. assistances given to Panchayats under the obligations of the Act one should not wonder when it came to merely 6¼ percent of total Land Revenue the Panchayats had collected on behalf of the State Govt. Compared to other States Bihar remained a state of ill-financed Panchayats 6¼ was the lowest amount given to them by the State Govt. The fate of even this source of income became controversial when there came the abolition of land revenue from uneconomic holdings of lands. Through another course of investigation it was empirically established that a Panchayat hardly earned 11 paise per capita annually out of the Land Revenue Commission.[4]

From what ever has been discussed above it becomes evidently clear that Panchayats' resources during initial days were not only alarming but were also disheartening when they were much expected to display their democratic identity in revolutionizing the socio-political scene. There was every truth in the observations of the Study Team on Panchayati Raj Finance that "there were Panchayats who were not discharging even the minimum obligatory function largely due to the paucity of funds. Even the basic civic amenities like safe drinking water supply, sanitation and conservancy were not provided to the community.[5] Finding the Panchayats no where standing before the Municipality S.C. Jain while expressing his concern had said "... if rural urban disparity is adopted as a basic requirements of social justice, the citizens of the rural areas would be under served unless the present income and expenditure level is raised ten times its present level.[6]

About the role played by the village Panchayats in the development administration the Study Team appointed by the Committee on Plan Project had observed : the available information indicates that possibly not more than 10 percent of the total number of Panchayats are functioning effectively, roughly ½ are average and the remaining about 40 percent are working unsatisfactorily ... the actual performance of Panchayats is generally limited to making arrangements for sanitation, conservancy, construction and repair of fair weather Roads, provision of domestic water supply and street lighting. Even these simple and elementary civic functions are not being performed with a degree of efficiency over large areas ... only small number of Panchayats those situated within or near the Block areas have shown a zeal for development activities on any appreciable scale.[7]

Explaining financial crisis facing Panchayats the Study Team of Committee on Plan Project had observed : "The Panchayats are generally handicapped for want of adequate financial resources to meet the growing expenditure on local programmes of development. It is evident that without financial assistance from the State Govt. many Panchayats cannot continue their existence. It would appear from the available data that the majority of working Panchayats over large areas have an annual income not exceeding Rs. 500/- from all resources including Govt. supply. Deducting the small establishments maintained by the Panchayats on account of pay of the Secretary who is whole time or part-time in many cases, conservancy staff, contingencies and contributions for the upkeep of Nyay Panchayats, very little is left for constructive and welfare activities. There are three major aspects of the problem relating to finance : inadequate resources allotted to Panchayats under the Acts, a general reluctance to make use of the existing resources and general inefficiency in tax administration. In the sphere of finance some of the difficulties are partly administrative and even temperamental. Not only Panchayats levy even compulsory taxes and fewer collect them with any degree of efficiency. In Bihar, Orissa and Madhya Pradesh, it is reliably learnt that the collection do not exceed 25-30 percent. In many cases sarpanchas and panchas are among the defaulters. The complaints of discriminations in assessment are fairly common and in a few cases a deliberative victimization. The assessment lists are not periodically reviewed. There is general aversion to adopt coercive measures, which, it is feared, will make the Panchayats unpopular. It is well to bear in mind that the general failure to assess and collect various taxes and fees has wider repercussions. It creates an atmosphere unfavourable to the growth of the Panchayats.[8]

Following the recommendations of the Study Team the Govt. of Bihar enacted the Bihar Panchayat Samitis and Zila Parishads Act 1961. Provisions made in the Act to make Panchayats economically viable units were quite crazy but Panchayats had to remain languishing financially and could not make it finance beyond 15 paise per head per year. This evidently shows that sincerity on the part of the Govt. to ensure smooth functioning of Panchayati Raj System has been doubtful and questions its commitment towards its own policy.

After the introduction of Panchayati Raj the Govt. started making a fuss about the revolutionary role assigned to the PRIS. but no sooner the scheme came into being the Govt. was exposed for its leap services paid to them. No effort was ever made to improve the situation of funding these institutions consequently the income pattern of Panchayat under the Bihar Act of 1961 remained where it was in 1947.[9] Nothing specific has ever been done to make these institutions effective by equipping financial resources etc. The only difference noticeable between the Panchayats under 1947 to that of 1961 Acts was the degree of importance that had been attached to them under the new provisions.[10] The Gram Panchayats in the State had a very weak financial base right from their inception. Inspite of various amendments made in the Panchayat Acts from time to time, these institutions were neither financially viable nor effective. There had been a provision to allot 6.25 percent or more of land revenue to Panchayats, but this revenue had never been made available and the Panchayats had been resorting to filing writ petitions against the State Govt. to secure their share. The Panchayats were also entitled to grants and loans from both the Centre and the State. They had the power to borrow from the cooperative banks or the State Panchayat Raj Finance Cooperation. The Gram Panchayats were also empowered to generate resources from tax, fee, etc. But they showed reluctance to utilize such financial powers.[11]

The Report of the Eleventh Finance Commission shows that the Panchayats' contribution in meeting out the revenue expenditure from their own sources almost through out the country is abysmally poor. This is evident from the fact that, during 1997-98, in 9 out of the 12 major states, Panchayats could meet not more than 10 percent of their revenue expenditure from their own resources. Panchayats are not even able to meet expenses towards maintenance of core services like Primary education, Primary health, drinking water supply, street lighting, sanitation and Roads. The NIRD study quoted by the Finance Commission indicates that the assessment of the requirement of funds has been at 225731 crore for a period of 5 years for rural local bodies, of which Rs. 142128 crore (63 percent of the total assessment is for operation and maintenance of these core services. In a nut-shell Panchayats' economies are 'grant-diet' economies. They are practically implementing the schemes handed over to them by the centre and states that too on dictated lines for rural people.[12] In a recent study of the working of the PRIS in 19 states, the NIRD found that there is a tendency to execute only schemes sponsored by the State or the Union Govts. Hardly, any programme is carried from PRIS. own resources.

The States complied with the constitutional provision of constituting the State Finance Commissions (SFCS), but did not provide them clear statement of spending responsibilities of the PRIS. This makes their recommendations inherently week.[13] "Many states have attached qualifying strings like "within the limits of its funds' "as far as Gram Panchayat funds at its disposal"; "to the extent its funds allow to perform". It means that availability of resources would determine their developmental role and not the vice-versa.[14]

Speaking in terms of Bihar, opportunity for employment, water facility, education, electricity, Road and health have been the core problems which have not shown any marked sign of improvement so far. For such a situation lack of financial powers to PRIS and non-cooperation from administration appear instrumental. Consequently it is almost 5 years of the Panchayats coming into being in its new avtar, however, its significance is hardly felt by the common people. As the situation stands, neither the integrated development nor the problems of farmers have hardly been sized up. Besides, non-transfer of powers to Panchayats brings about a deep sense of resentment among the elected representatives themselves. The growing lacks of enthusiasm among them evidently manifests when Panchayats' meetings are frequently dissolved for lack of quorum and in some cases meetings are not at all convened. When ever there takes place the meeting Governmental functionaries connected with rural development often absent themselves from the proceedings of the meetings. As a result of which it becomes impossible to take any decision prominently in the area of Education, Agricultural credit card to farmers, Bank loans, flood and draught relief- Irrigation and such other matter of great public interests.

Jobs transferred to Panchayats under the XIth schedule of the constitution had the underlying objectives that decentralized forms of administration procedure will be simplified which will ultimately go in the larger interests of the public. But indifferences so far shown by the Govt. functionaries have deterred any radical transformation. Through welfare schemes people of other states are generally benefited where as in Bihar because of rampant corruption and lack of enthusiasm among the functionaries (both Govt. and public) the wheel of development remains statis.[15] As per the spirit of the Bihar Panchayat Raj Act, officers placed with development activities should have bequeathed their powers to the PRIS but these functionaries neither relinquished their powers nor they did any thing on their own to improve the situation. If things are allowed to go unchanged neither there can be any development in the State nor the farmers will be able to derive any considerable benefit out of the various projects meant for them.

Looking into the actual status of Panchayat in terms of Funds let us go back to the provisions made in the Bihar Panchayat Raj Act, 1993. Section 26 of the Act says "A Gram Panchayat shall have power to acquire, hold and dispose of property and enter into contract provided that in all cases of disposal of immovable property by the Panchayat it shall obtain the prior approval of the Govt.

1. All properties within the local limits of the jurisdiction of Gram Panchayat other than property maintained by the central or the State Govt. or a local authority or any other Gram Panchayat, shall vest in and belong to the Gram Panchayat and shall with all other property of whatsoever nature or kind which may become vested in the Gram Panchayat, under its direction, management and control that is to say:

    a) All general properties;

    b) All public streets, including the soil, stones and other materials thereof and all drain, bridges, culverts, trees, erection material, implements and other things provided for such streets;

    c) All public channels, water courses, springs, tanks, ghats, reservoirs cisterns, wells, aqueducts, conduits, tunnels, pipes, pumps and other water works whether made, laid or erected at the cost of the Gram Panchayat or otherwise, and all bridges, buildings, engines, works, materials, and things connected there with or appertaining there to and also any adjacent land (not being private property) appertaining to any public tank;

d) All public sewers and drains and all works, materials and things appertaining thereto and other conservancy works;

e) All sewage, rubbish and offensive matter deposited on streets or collected by the Gram Panchayat from streets, latrines, urinals, sewers, cesspools and other places.

f) All public lamps, lamp posts and apparatus connected there with or appertaining there to; and

g) All buildings erected by the Gram Panchayat and all lands and buildings or the property transferred to the Gram Panchayat by the Central or the State Govt. or acquired by gift, purchase or otherwise for local public purposes.

2. The Govt. may allocate to a Gram Panchayat any public property situated within it's local jurisdiction and thereupon such property shall vest in and come under the control of the Gram Panchayat.

All these should constitute property of a Gram Panchayat with a scope of generating income by initiative and a sense of doing some concrete things to justify their existence.

Besides allocation of these properties to the Panchayats the State Govt. have constituted a Gram Panchayat Fund and there shall be placed to the credit thereof.

a) Contributions and Grants, if any, made by the Central or the State Govt;

b) Contribution and Grants, if any, made by the Zila Parishad, Panchayat Samiti or any other local authority;

c) Loans, if any, granted by the Central or the State Govts;

d) All receipts on accounts of taxes, rates and fees levied by it;

e) All receipts in respect of any schools, hospitals, dispensaries, buildings, institutions, or works vested in or constructed by or placed under the control and management of the Gram Panchayat;

f) All sums received by or on behalf of the Gram Panchayat;

g) Such fines and penalties imposed and realized under the provisions of this Act as may be prescribed; and

h) All other sums received by or on behalf of the Gram Panchayat.

We have now seen the latest legal provisions providing scope to Gram Panchayats not only for generation of income out of the properties allocated to them under the Act but also for management of funds at their disposal.

We, on our part, had to look into such aspects by contracting Panchayats' functionaries within Naugachia Sub-division, the universe of our study. It is surprising to know that none, neither the ward members nor the Mukhias had ever heard about creation of Panchayat funds either at the initiative of State Govt. functionaries or they themselves. If they ever heard about it, it was apparently from us only when all of them, say cent percent of them expressed their unawareness about the provision of constituting Panchayat Fund within the provisions of the Act. What we could comprehend from their level of unawareness is that Panchayats have, every time, been built upon "Grant-Diet" concept and never on the ethics of "Self-help". They have yet to learn lessons in self-help only then they would be able to realise their responsibility of raising funds to be tapped from sources allocated to them under the provision of the Act.

NOTES AND REFERENCES

1.   Local Finance Enquiry Committee (1951), Para- 131, pp. 294-95, Govt. of India Publications.

2.   Sec. 4-11, p. 12 of the Report of the Study Team on Panchayati Raj Finance (1963), Govt. of India, Ministry of C.D. and Cooperation.

3.   G.N. Thakur, Op.Cit., pp. 126-27.

4.   G.N. Thakur, Op.Cit., p. 1.

5.   Sec. 3-12, p. 9, of the Report of the Study Team on P.R. Finance (1963), GOI.

6.   S.C. Jain- Community Development and Panchayati Raj inIndia (1967), Allied Publishers, p. 226.

7.   Sec. 2-3, Vol. I of the Report of the Committee on Plan Project (1957).

8.   Sec. 33, Vol. I of the Report of the Committee on Plan Project (1957).

9.   G.N. Thakur, Op.Cit., p. 131.

10.   G.N. Thakur, Op.Cit., p. 131.

11.   K.K. Sinha- "Evolution of P.R. in Bihar", Kurukshetra, Sept. 2001, p. 42.

12.   Mahipal- "Role of Panchayats in Rural Reconstruction"- Yojna, Jan. 2002, p. 61.

13.   Rajesh K. Jha- "Panchayats- Story of Promises and Pitfalls"- Kurukshetra, Jan. 2004, pp. 40-44.

14.   Rajesh K. Jha, Ibid, p. 40.

15.   Editorial Dainik Jagran (Bhagalpur), dt. 19.9.2004.

LEADERSHIP PERCEPTION OF THE ROLE OF OFFICIALS ATTACHED TO PANCHAYATI RAJ BODIES

Panchayats have been institutions of village governance since time immemorial. During the ancient period Panchayats were operative for just settlement of inter-village and intra-village disputes. India has probably the oldest tradition of local institution of governance. Panchayats were also a unit of local administration since the early British regime, but they had to function under Govt. control. When the Indian freedom fighters demanded for democratization of the colonial structure, the British Govt. responded by offering concessions at the lowest level initially by delegating powers of self Govt. to Panchayats in the rural areas and to municipalities in urban areas. Without retracing the detailed evolution of local self Govt. it to relevant to state here that "they were structurally and functionally different from the traditional communitarian Panchayats of Indian villages whose forte was maintenance of customs ... while the new institutions were local executive agencies for implementation of national/provincial policies with negligible element of local democratic or bureaucratic autonomy.[1]

By the Govt. of India Act of 1935, the power to enact legislation on local Govt. was entrusted to the provincial legislatures. By virtue of this power, new Acts were enacted by many states vesting power of administration including criminal justice in the hands of Panchayats. Panchayats and their functions were perceived as the least important by the colonial regime. Under the British rule, these institutions were entrenched in the colonial logic of obeisance to empire and as far as rural India was concerned (those Panhayats) could not make interventions to bring about a rural transformation.

Post 1947 was a period of euphoria of freedom. The main preoccupations of the first few Govts. were political stability, poverty alleviation and rapid development. Provincial Govts. enacted laws to establish local body institutions with varying patterns from single tier to three tiers. But these institutions were far from being effective.

The Balwant Rai Mehta Committee (1957) which was mandated to study and report on the Community Development Programme (C.D.P) and the National Extension Service (N.E.S) examined aspects pertaining to improvement in social and economic conditions in rural India and utilization of local initiative as envisaged under the two schemes. The Committee etched out a decisive role for the Panchayats beginning with recommendations for devolution of powers and programme planning. The nature of this institutional functioning was outlined as participatory.[2]

A change from police state to welfare state that India is mandated to adopt requires far reaching changes in the administrative was machinery which unfortunately, was not immediately realised by the enthusiastic nationalist Govt. Instead of bringing any change in the system, the local system of governance through institutional arrangement for transformation of rural situation was sudden, quick and wide spread through out the country. The traditional bureaucratic set up was now called upon to undertake the gigantic task of nation building about which it had neither previous experience nor competence. In other words, the administrative standard was almost the same as was until 1947. Till the other day of the Panchayati Raj Scheme the impression was vocal among the people that the Govt. agency was not transferring initiative and leadership to people's agency and their leaders which considerably hampered the growth of self-reliance among the people and this caused their dependence more and more on Govt. and its agencies. There have been also a wide spread feeling among the people that Govt. servants were deliberately keeping most of the powers in their own hands and they were not willing to part with those powers and prestige which they were now forced to do. The Report of the Committee on Democratic Decentralisation set up by the Maharastra Govt. observed : "In past, the administrative machinery had to play a dominant role in framing policies and their execution. In recent times, progressively, the policy functions have passed on to the elected representatives at grass root level also particularly after the Panchayati Raj System came into being. This has been interpreted in some quarters as a process of some body wresting power and authority from others. In fast changing situation it is natural on the part of the officials to develop a feeling of contempt and resentment against those who have come to take their powers. Suddenness of debureaucratization with corresponding loss of power and authority is likely to create deep strains in the officials' minds. Such stress and strains are likely to be reflected in their attitude towards the non-officials over whom they have lost their powers to rule." They still believe in the efficiency of traditional approach to administration. New approaches are half heartedly adopted. It is rightly said that traditions die hard. Does this not apply with the bureaucratic traditions also? This is not without substantial reasons. Some such reasons may be like.

They are trained in the same high standard of administrative glamour and pride as had been the case with the I.A.S. trainees if not the I.C.S. They are trained in the typical British colonial administrative pattern to rule over the people, its essential feature being the maintenance of distance and creation of awe in the minds of the people which is essential for the maintenance of Law and order. As against this the democratic decentralisation has raised in people's minds expectations of radical change in the role of Govt. servants and in their attitude and behaviour. They are not only now asked to compromise their schooled judgement about administration but also to suffer some loss in the elite status for which they were trained. This is quite painful for them.

Officers functioning in Panchayats and also its other higher organs are drawn from state civil services and are on deputation for a fixed period in Panchayati Raj bodies in whatever capacity.

Besides, each and every staff from Panchayat's Gram Sewak to the Zila Parishad's secretary are all recruited under the conditions laid down by the State Govt. for such recruitments Panchayat Raj bodies having nothing to do in the process. Because of the nature of their deputation in Panchayati Raj services those officers not having job satisfaction spend their time on Panchayati Raj duties as a period of interlude which one has to get over during the course of one's career. Therefore, for them to be on deputation in Panchayati Raj services is just a compulsion and not an incentive which does not make the job attracting for him/her.

A dual line of control has replaced the single line of allegiance Administrative hierarchy is still a rule rather an exception. The dual allegiance has resulted in complete division of loyalty of these officers so much so that the element of spirit behind securing the association of Govt. controlled officers is entirely defeated and purpose remains unfulfilled. What these officers generally are found doing is that they give priority to the orders of their departmental bosses than these elected representatives who equally claim to be their boss which leads to not only to a conflicting situation but that of the situation of chaos and uncertainty. Such a dual control had been termed by Chetkar Jha "indefensible". At another place he had said "these officers are placed in an awkward position when they have to look up to two matters."[3]

Introduction of the scheme of Panchayati Raj adopted through out the country after the Balwant Rai Mehta's Report in early sixties had signaled the changing role of the offers and officials to be attached with the new scheme of rural administration where they had to encounter new challenges. Under the new system people's representatives were associated every where in dominating positions. Devolution of powers to people's representatives at local level had necessitated during those days also a reorientation of administrative outlook and reorganisation of relationship with people's representatives at each level. These officers were also then expected to perform a set of novel and different jobs than they were doing before. The emerging situation was sure to bring superiority of people's representatives over these officers. A Parmukh of the Panchayat Samiti was supposed to write the annual confidential report of the B.D.O. who also happened to be the Executive Officer of the Panchayat Samiti. Officers were normally supposed to guide the deliberations of the meetings presided over by the elected leadership and to execute what ever was decided at such meetings by the non-official members in order to keep them within legal frame work. But the right to advise, as also supported by S.C. Jain[4] does not mean official interference in policy matters, because the final acceptance or rejection of the alternatives was the prerogative of the non official leadership."

The 73rd Amendment of the Indian Constitution besides bringing other new changes in the Panchayati Raj system, through article 243 G. of the constitution empowered the State Legislatures to endow Panchayats with such powers and authority as may be necessary to enable theme to function as institutions of self Govt. The article also contained provisions for the devolution of powers and delegation of responsibilities upon Panchayats at the appropriate level for preparation of plans for economic development and social justice including those in relation to the matters listed in the XIth schedule of the constitution. The XIth schedule of the constitution contains a list of 29 subjects relating to agriculture, poverty alleviation, education including cultural activities, health and family welfare, welfare of weaker sections and maintenance of community assets.

Late Narsimha Rao, the then Prime Minister of India, while writing a letter to the Sarpanches of the country after the 73rd Amendment of the constitution had stated : Thus you would be glad to know that democracy and devolution of powers to Panchayats have now become part of the most sacred document of this nation : the constitution of India. No one can now snatch democratic practices from your Panchayat, Panchayats cannot be arbitrarily suspended or dissolved now. No one will be able to take away the powers, responsibilities and finances devolved upon the Panchayats. the constitutional changes will prove to be a major landmark in the history of development of rural areas of this country.

This Act will ensure that real power will go back to you only and you will be expected to play a much greater role in the development of your area and people ... village Panchayats will very soon become living institutions on permanent basis and will consist of representatives of the people elected by them. These institutions will run various programmes for their welfare and will also involve people in their planning. They will be vibrant institutions performing necessary development, regulatory and general administrative functions Agriculture, land improvement, Animal husbandry, village and cottage industries, drinking water, poverty alleviation programmes, Health, Sanitation, Family welfare etc. will necessarily be the concern of the village Panchayats. They must be able to provide for the day to day common needs of the people besides protecting their well-being in different ways ..."[5] This is how the process of empowerment of Panchayats was further initiated accelerated.

Article 243 G. included in this part, provides that these institutions shall be given the power to levy, collect and appropriate certain taxes, duties, tolls and fees and would also be getting grants-in-aids from the consolidated funds of the states to enable them to perform these responsibilities. In addition to it, provision was made in it for the establishment of State Finance Commission for distributing proceeds of the taxes, duties, tolls and fees levied by the State Govt. between them and the PRIS. for this purpose.

We have number of Programmes and schemes for rural development. From both, central and State Govts. considerable budgetary resources are being allocated to them. Both non-officials and officials of the PRIS. are the instruments to invest these resources in fruitful and effective way for the development of masses. But the experience so far gained revealed that even after a decade of functioning of Panchayats both officials and non-officials don't have their role clarity at institutional level and there still exists the chaos by way of both of the functionaries not getting along for one or the other reason more on personal reasons. There was the need for better coordination between the PRIS. and bureaucracy for speedy development of rural areas.

The elected representatives were also expected to widen their vision of progress and improve their capabilities. Awareness is needed not just among the rural populace but also among the Panchayat representatives. Their strength will help implement development schemes at the ground level. It is with this spirit that Panchayat representatives are supposed to develop functional relationship with the officers and officials associated with the system. The role of these functionaries were to be appreciated at length by the elected representatives in these bodies. The bureaucrats in the system were equally responsible for the smooth functioning of these institutions. It is relevant to add here that the constitution of India has always visualised the PRIS. as the unit of self Govt. (Art. 40) and later on as the institution of self Govt. articles 243 (d) and 243 (G). It is remarkable that the seventy third constitutional Amendment emphasizes on Panchayats to be institution itself, rather than being units merely. This entails functional and financial autonomy along with accountable personnel at its disposal.

In a recent study of the working of the PRIS the National Institute for Rural Development (NIRD), however, found that there is a tendency to execute only schemes sponsored by the state or the union Govt. Hardly any programme is carried from PRI's own resources. For such a situation both, the elected representatives and the governmental functionaries are equally responsible. So long PRIS. do not have schemes of their own they can't justify their existence vis-a-vis a hostile governmental apparatus.

Recently the Task Force of the Ministry of Rural Development on the PRIS had observed : The functions devolved upon PRIS are in the nature of 'subjects' rather than in terms of activities. The role ambiguity of the PRIS is not only transgression of principles of sound management, but hindrance to their efficiency and effectiveness also.

Before jumping to a definite conclusion about the perception of local leadership in relation to bureaucracy like deployed in the system of Panchayati Raj, we feel like discussing what changes have been statutorily brought about in relation to the role of officers and officials associated with the latest edition of   Panchayati Raj compared to the status of their counterparts in its earlier incarnations in the context of Bihar where Panchayati Raj as a concept was institutionalised through its enactment- The Bihar Panchayat Samiti and Zila Parishads Act 1961. Constitutional status to the latest edition of Panchayati Raj system having been granted through the 73rd Amendment of the constitution, the Bihar Govt. also followed suit by enacting Bihar Panchayati

Raj Act,1993 which was supposed to convey the elements of constitutional recognition to the Panchayati Raj system in its new Avtar.

About the earlier edition of Panchayati Raj the association of officers and officials in the system came to be subjected to various controversies weakening on the very credibility of the system. There came moments when presence of non-officials members in dominating position in the system was an eye sore for the officers from the Govt. It was more temperamental than administrative or any thing else. No one particular reason was responsible for the tense relationship existed between these two sets of functionaries. At best we can refer back to Laski's observation in this particular sphere when he said "the relationship between the elected members and the expert is not susceptible of definitions. It is a habit of mind, a tradition which can be recognised when seen but eludes the printed world". Besides it was temperamental the luke warm policy of the State Govt. towards decentralisation of powers to the PRIS was very much responsible for development of a tense relationship between both sets of functionaries. For example,

a)   Recruitment of the officers and officials being associated with the system was the prerogative of the State Govt.

b)   Absence of PR. cadres for them : those associated in the system were having their departmental cadre intact while their deputation in PR. services;

c)   Dual allegiance : Instead of a single line allegiance these officers were subjected to dual line of allegiance paying greater attention to their departmental dictates and lesser for that of Panchayati Raj leadership.

All these factors when taken together made the officers and officials associated with Panchayati Raj bodes not only contemptuous against elected bosses in the system but also sometime aggresive. So its was a situation of virtual stand off. In the words of the committee on Democratic Decentralisation set up by the Govt. of Maharstra "In the past the administrative machinery had to play a dominant role in framing policies and their execution. In recent times, progressively, policy function has rightly passed on to the elected representatives of the people. This has been interpreted in some quarters as a process of somebody wresting power and authority from others. In such fast changing situation it is natural on the part of the officials to develop a feeling of contempt and resentment against those who have come to take over their powers. Suddenness of debureacratisation with corresponding loss of power and authority is likely to create deep strains in the officials. Such stress and strains are likely to be reflected in their attitudes towards the non-officials over whom they have lost their powers to 'rule'."

With the enforcement of the Bihar Panchayati Raj Act 1993, the Govt. of Bihar in pursuance of the spirit of the 73rdconstitutional Amendment once again delegated but not decentralized functions of 29 departments including

i)   Agriculture,

ii)   Revenue

iii)   Water Management (Minor Irrigation),

iv)   Animal husbandry and fisheries,

v)   Public Health Engineering,

vi)   Rural Development Dept,

vii)   Energy Dept,

viii)   Primary and Adult Education,

ix)   Secondary, Primary and Adult Education,

x)   Arts, Culture and Sports,

xi)   Health, Medical, Education and Family welfare,

xii)   Welfare Department,

xiii)   Social welfare Dept,

xiv)   Labour, Employment and Training,

xv)   Food, Supply and Commerce

xvi)   Relief and rehabilitation Dept.

All such decisions were taken in a separate compendium issued by the Directorate of Panchayati Raj, Rural Development Department in October 2001 with a clear noting ^^;|fi f=Lrjh; iapk;rksa }kjk vius lalk/kuksa ls lafo/kku X;kjgoh vuqlwph esa of.kZr fo"k;ksa ds vUrxZr ;kstukvksa dk lq=.k dksbZ ck/kk ugha gS] ijUrq O;kogkfjd n`f"Vdks.k ls dbZ ekeyksa esa ,slk laHko ugha gks ikrk gS] pwafd vko';drkvksa dh rqyuk esa vkfFkZd lalk/kuksa dh deh gSA lafo/kku dh frgÙkjosa la'kks/ku dh Hkkouk ds vuq:i ifj;kstukvksa ds dk;ZUo;u esa f=Lrjh; iapk;rksa dh dkjxj lgHkkfxrk lqfuf'pr djus ds fy;s ;g vko';d gks tkrk gS fd ljdkj ds fofHkUu foHkkxksa ds ekStwnk dk;ZØeksa@ ifj;kstukvksa dk lQy lesdu iapk;r jkt O;oLFkk ds lkFk fd;k tk;A**

The above noting manifests the intention of the Govt. expressing its inability to transfer complete powers to the PRIS in accordance with the spirit of the 73rd Amendment more because of financial strains. However the Govt. of Bihar decided to go along with PRIS. in the matters of these departments by way of seeking their collaboration in one way or the other and not to rush for complete transfer of powers relating to these departments as such.

Govt's intention in not transferring complete powers to PRIS, by implications, gives strength to the continuance of officialdom in matters of both policy making and also implementation thereof.

The reluctance on the part of State Govts. to transfer powers to PRIS. was highlighted during the proceedings of All India Conference of the heads of Panchayats, at New Delhi in early 2002. Representatives present there expressed simmering discontent over the half-hearted implementation of the constitutional provisions of PRIS. So the point that remains unanswered is that even after a decade or so of the 73rd amendment of the constitution, are the Panchayats merely paper tigers? A closer scrutiny of the states of devolution of powers to Panchayats in the last 12 years bears the testimony of the state's reluctance and a bumpy road ahead for grass root democracy in India.

Recently the Task Force of the Ministry of Rural Development on the PRIS observed : "The functions devolved upon PRIS are in the nature of 'subjects' rather than in terms of 'activities' or 'sub-activities'. This role ambiguity of the PRIS is not only transgression of principles of sound management, but hindrance to their efficiency and effectiveness also.[6]

Contrary to the prevailing situation, the Indian constitution has always visualised the PRIS as the unit of Self Govt. (Article- 40) and later on as the institution of self Govt. [Articles 243 (d) and 243 (G)]. It is remarkable that the seventy third amendment emphasises on Panchayats to be institutions itself, rather than being units merely. This entails functional and financial autonomy along with accountable personnel at its disposal. Articles 243 G. and 243 H. provide these autonomies, but the extent and scope of the autonomies are left to the discretion of the states which have never been well disposed with these local level institutions for which they are constitutionally obliged not only for their empowerment but also their full growth with strength.

How is the perception of Panchayat level leaders in regard to the extent of availability of a accountable personnel at its disposal is a point we have tried to ascertain from the sample of respondents themselves by putting them a specific question to this effect which ran : ^^iapk;r lfpo ds vfrfjDr vU; dbZ iz[kaM@ ftyk Lrjh; vf/dkjh dks iapk;r ds v/khu py jgs fodkl dk;ksZ esa de ls de rdfudh lg;ksx nsus dk izko/kku gSA iapk;r dks bu vf/dkfj;ksa ls visf{kr lg;ksx fey ikrk gS vFkok ugha\

gka@ugha@ugha tkurs]

;fn ugha rks dkj.k crkosa**

Out of the total 97 respondents we had in or sample 23 said 'yes'- 12 aid 'No' and 62 said 'Don't know'. While analysing the response categories we should bear in mind that Panchayats are yet more or less, treated as executing agencies of schemes sponsored by the state or the union Govt. They have in terms of personnel, a whole time a secretary paid by the Govt. who is responsible for maintaining records of Panchayat besides assisting the Panchayat executive. While acting as the executing agent of either the state or the union Govt. the Panchayat or Zila

Parishad as the case might be through their respective personnel extends necessary technical/administrative assistance for the specific purposes of execution of schemes and keeping things within specifications. This is why role of officials in Panchayat is not pronounced as it is the case with a Panchayat Samiti or Zila Parishad where there is a net work of Govt. functionaries of different categories responsible for giving assistance and advise both in the matters of policy making and execution thereof also.

Besides , presence of officials is felt more by the Mukhia of the Panchayat than ward members. It is the Mukhia who is accountable for the execution of schemes and not the ordinary members. So response in 'yes' category is more of Mukhias and that of in 'DK' category relates to the ward members- who are in no way accountable for the execution unless he or she is appointed as an executing agent- which hardly occurs.

NOTES AND REFERENCES

1.   P.C. Mathur- "The constitutional Panchayats of India – some Emerging Jurico-philosophical issues" in S.P. Jain and Thomas W Hothgesang Emerging Trend in Panchayati Raj (Rural Local Self Govt. in India) Ed. 1995.

2.   Feernandes Aureliano- reconnecting Sabha to Gram in strengthening village Democracy R.C. Choudhary and S.P. Jain (ed) (1999), NIRD.

3.   Chetakar Jha – His article on "Circumstances of Leadership at Block Level."

4.   See S.C. Jain, Op.Cit, p. 409.

5.   Kurukshetra- June, 1993, p. 5-6.

6.   Aureliano Fernandes- "Changing Role of Panchayats in the New Millennium"- Kurukshetra, Nov. 2001, p. 40.

LEADERSHIP PERCEPTION OF OVERALL CONSTRAINTS IN THE WORKING OF THE SYSTEM

The Institution of Panchayat was seldom born out of conviction and passion and as the only sure means of developing rural India. It was always by way of option. Post 1947 was a period tinged with euphoria of freedom. Provincial Govts. enacted laws to establish local body institutions with varying patterns from single tier to three tiers. It is out of this enthusiasm that a study team under the leadership of Balwant Rai Mehta was constituted by the Committee on Plan Project (1957) to study and Report on the Community Development Programme and the National Extension Service. The study team examined aspects pertaining to improvement in social and economic conditions in rural India and utilization of local initiative as envisaged under the two schemes. The Committee etched out a decisive role for the Panchayats beginning with devolution of power and programme planning. The nature of this institutional functioning was outlined as participatory.

The Committee offered two directional thrusts (a) administrative decentralisation for effective implementation of development programmes, (b) Decentralisation of the administrative system under the control of local bodies. The initial decentralisation package, in the wake of the acceptance of the recommendations of the committee on plan project, however began to shrink as soon as Pt. Nehru died in 1964- who had thrown his weight behind Panchayat to confer on it the responsibility of management of development programmes. By 1970 things deteriorated very much with Panchayat system with the State and Central Political elites paying little attention towards the PRIS. (Also see Mathur,1995 : 9) with Nehru going behind the scene the euphoria of democratic decentralisation, a loudly proclaimed national policy started showing sign of decline particularly due to lack of state support to this phenomenon. Decentralisation was the sole concern of the Central Govt. was taken to be an act of the Central Govt. where in the State powers found greater scope of their being sidelined, therefore states hostility towards this concept of decentralisation was not therefore without a conspiracy. .

The issue once again was revived during the incumbency of Rajiv Gandi who had tried to bring a new shape to the PRIS. through out the country. The 64th Amendment Bill which sought to give constitutional status to PRIS introduced by Rajiv Gandhi was defeated in Parliament apparently due to stiff opposition from state leaders in an apprehension that if PRIS are truly effective there would be chances of usurpation of powers of the states. With these misgivings PRIS could not grow on desired lines. It ultimately remained the victim of plethora of illusions and confusions. They pitifully failed to secure the sympathy of the State Govts., instead got its hostility. Notwithstanding the hostile attitude of the State powers the Panchayati Raj concept could not extinguish for what ever reason.

During the period of Late Narsimha Rao, the then Prime Minister of India, Panchayati Raj was again brought into focus. It was during this period that the 73rd amendment of the Indian Constitution was passed in the Parliament. As a result of which democracy and devolution of powers to Panchayats became the part of the constitution. The 73rd Amendment ensured regular elections of Panchayats, provided adequate representation of S.Sc, S.Ts. and women as members. Besides, Article 243 G. of the constitution empowers the State legislatures to endow Panchayats with such powers and authority as may be necessary to enable them to functions as institutions of Self Govt. The Article also contains provisions for the devolution of powers and delegation of responsibility upon Panchayats at the appropriate level for preparation of plans for economic development and social justice including those in relation to the matters listed in the XIth schedule of the constitution. The XIth Schedule of the constitution contains a list of 29 subjects relating to agriculture, poverty alleviation, education including cultural activities, health and family welfare, welfare of weaker sections and maintenance of community assets.

The Amendment Act created an impression that PRIS. would necessarily be empowered. It inserted part IX of the constitution. Article 243 G. of this part made the provision that the states 'may' devolve powers and authority on these bodies to make them institutions of Self Govt. It also provided that PRIS. may also be given powers pertaining to 29 subjects listed in the Eleventh Schedule for making and implementing plans for economic development and social justice.

Article 243 included in this part provides that these institutions shall be given the powers to levy, collect and appropriate certain taxes, duties, tolls and fees and would also be getting grants-in-aid from the consolidated fund of the states to enable them to perform these responsibilities. In addition to it, provision was made for the establishment of State Finance Commissions for distributing proceeds of the taxes, duties, tolls and fees levied by the State Govts. between them and the PRIS for the purpose.

The 73rd amendment Act has, as we can see, made Panchayats an institution of Self Govt. Although the term "institution" of Self Govt. has not been defined in the Act, the connotation is well understood, viz.

a) Institutional existence i.e, the decisions are taken by the people's representatives,

b) Institutional capacity i.e. the institution is empowered to make rules independently, and

c) Financial viability i.e. it is sufficiently empowered to raise financial resources to meet its responsibilities.

In other words, Panchayats should enjoy functional, administrative and financial autonomy. Article 243 G. of the constitution envisaged Panchayats as institution of Self Govt. which means they should enjoy functional, financial and administrative autonomy in their working.[1]

The constitution has had always visualised the PRIS as the unit of Self Govt. (Art. 40) and later on as the institution of Self Govt. [Articles 243 (d) and 243 (G)]. The 73rd Amendment emphasizes on Panchayats to be institution itself, rather than being units merely. This entails functional and financial autonomy along with accountable personnel at its disposal. Articles 243 G. and 243 H. provide these autonomies, but the extent and scope of the autonomies are left to the direction of the states. (The use of 'may' in these articles is very deceptive in this regard). and overall track record of the states has been very dismal in fulfilling spirit and expectations of even the constitution if they ask for parting with its powers. Only two states (Karnatak and Sikkim) have brought personnel related to all 29 subjects under the jurisdiction of the PRIS. Other states have not transferred any personnel to PRIS.[2] That is why the National Commission to review the working of the constitution (NCRWC) suggested to make the provision mandatory for the states by recommending this new version of the Article 243 G. "subject to the provisions of the constitution the Legislature of the State shall, by Law vest the Panchayats with such powers and authority as are necessary to enable them to function as institution of Self Govt. and such Law shall contain provisions for the devolution of powers and responsibilities upon Panchayats at the appropriate level subject to such conditions as shall be specified therein, with respect to :

a)   Preparation of plans for economic development and social justice;

b)   The implementation of schemes for economic development and social justice as shall be entrusted to them including those in relation to the matter list in the Eleventh Schedule.[3]

A closer state wise scrutiny of the functioning of the PRIS suggest that effective decentralisation needs looking beyond the constitution. Contrary to it, the states like Bihar, Assam, Arunachal Pradesh, Jharkhand, Goa and Gujarat have not invested the transfer of any 3 F.S. (Funds, Functions and Functionaries) to the PRIS.[4]

After initial excitement of seventy third Amendment, the movement for decentralisation has now reached plateau. The elections have been held. The institutions of Panchayati Raj are in place and breathing. But the devolution of 3 FS. to the lowest tier is intangible. And the State Govts. are held the real villain in subverting the constitutional provisions in letter and spirit.[5]

During the proceedings of the All India Conference of the heads of Panchayats at New Delhi in early 2002 representatives present there expressed simmering discontent over the half hearted Implementation of the constitutional provision of PRIS. Recently the Task Force of the Ministry of Rural Development on the PRIS observed "the functions devolved upon PRIS are in nature of 'subjects', rather than in terms of 'activities' or 'sub-activities'. This role ambiguity of the PRIS is not only transgression of principles of sound management, but hindrance to their efficiency and effectiveness also. In the given situation, it was right on the part of the National Institution for

Rural Development to have observed in course of a recent study that "there is tendency (among the Panchayats) to execute only schemes sponsored by the State or the Union Govt. Hardly any programme is carried from PRIS own resources." This drives home the truth that in absence of autonomy to enable them to work independentally independent of the State Powers how one could expect a Panchayat to tackle the problems of the villages in their own way. Viewed from their level of performances, what we find to our great surprise is that there is hardly a Panchayat in Bihar which could provide even minimum basic facilities to its constituents, be it creating opportunity for employment, water facility, education, electricity, Road and health which the various Acts from time to time have had enjoined on the Govt. The reason for non-performance or not being accountable to its responsibilities towards the people living in its jurisdiction is not far to seek. The commonly pronounced reason for such a state of their inertia is the lack of funds for which they wait for grants from state or national Govt. as they preponderantly believed in 'Grant Diet' economy more than resorting to raising their own resources.

It will be unfair to singularly charge the State Govt. for not creating a sound financial position for them. The general reluctance on the part of Panchayats themselves to raise their own funds by collection of taxes they are authorised to levy is a great lapse on their part. The general failure to assess and collect taxes and fees has wider repercussions. It not only creates an atmosphere unfavourable to its own growth rather admits its own infirmities in securing a sound footing for itself.

Panchayats are supposed to be the pillar of Grass-Roots Democracy to be brought through the element of decentralisation and debureaucratisation. However to justify its position a Panchayat does not have anything of its own. Neither it has cultivated the image consciousness nor has it cared to cope with its own accountabilities. It does not apparently have the genuine concern to come to the expectations of its own constituents who expect fulfillment of their basic needs as the minimum. From what we have gathered through our own observations is that most of the Panchayats are contented to serve as the conduit of the State Govt. and has learnt to survive by merely implementing schemes handed over to them by the centre and the State Govts. With the constitution of the present Panchayat there was some sort of upsurge here and there to seek transfer of powers from the State Govt. and for that purpose at every Block level Mukhia Sangh was organized to put combined pressure on the Govt. but this too failed to yield any positive result thanks to the recalcitrant attitude of the State Govt. State Govt., by design, keeps the Panchayats in a State of perpetual chaos and succeeds through its administrative apparatus which weaken them to the extent that they could not become assertive and could also not become capable of being an institution with autonomy in the areas of Funds, Functions and Functionaries-the 3 FS. The State Govt. as things appear lacks the conscience to implement the spirit of the constitution, particularly the spirit of the 73rd amendment.

There is no gain saying that constitutional mandate envisaging empowerment of Panchayats still suffers from 'Dependency Syndrome' and Grass-root democracy thus envisaged through Panchayat "Little village Republic" remains a far cry. Besides, the element of distrust prevailing at the governmental level has further enmeshed the cause of grass-roots democracy.

For such a disquieting situation what we have found out is that lack of financial powers and administrative non-cooperation are at its roots. Money in the form of Grants is never timely released by the Grant giving authorities. During this span of 5 years almost, after the last election, Panchayats have not begun discharging even their minimum legal responsibilities. Besides, for the people, Panchayats are becoming the seat of corrupt practices and they also don't see any chance of its redemption. Employment, water facility, education, electricity, road and health were to be the core areas where Panchayats were called upon to improve with their newly acquired powers, but so far hardly there came any marked sign of initiative into our sight. For all such aberrations creeping into the system of Panchayats absence of political will is also greatly responsible. Missing political will joined by hostile bureaucracy adds fuel to the fire.

Both non-officials and officials associated with the system were to be the instruments to ensure proper growth of the system by way of deliverance and effectiveness. Cordial relationship between people's representatives and officers/officials is a prerequisite for the success of the system. However, the Panchayati Raj leadership appears to be obsessed of non-cooperative behaviour of the governmental agencies within the system. They (officials) do not observe transparency in most of the matters including availability of funds and resources according to the elected representatives. with such a colossal attitude on their parts, the people's representatives can't move forward and seriously formulate plans and policies according to the local needs. Jobs transferred to a Panchayat under the XIth schedule of the constitution had the underlying objectives that decentralized forms of administrative procedures will be simplified which will ultimately go in the larger inserts of the public. But indifferences so far shown by the State Govt. functionaries appear to have almost thwarted the prospects of the system of Panchayati Raj.

Such gaps, which are almost deliberate and under a design, have taken the toll of the system which has not only lost the element of self confidence within itself but also facing crisis of dignity. In this context the findings of the National Institute of Rural Development (NIRI) about the working of the PRIS is worth quoting here.

The study points out that "there is a tendency among Panchayats to execute only schemes sponsored by the union and the State Govts." This by implication suggests that Panchayats are left with no element of self-confidence and the zest to do something on its own is lost over. It is now obvious that inadequacies in the system of PR. flows from the lack of faith in the system by the State powers, emaciated by scanty resources and meager responsibilities. Evidently, the State Govt. is lacking in conscience to promote Panchayati Raj in pursuance of the spirit of the constitution of the country.

As per the Bihar Panchayat Raj Act 1993, officers and departments dealing with development matters were to withdraw their hobnobbing to pave for the empowerments of PRIS but neither they have withdrawn from hobnobbing with the system nor have they allowed the situation to change in favour of empowerment. Status-quo approach pursued by these vested interests creates a chaotic situation for PRIS. In other words such a tendency on the part of the governmental agencies is deemed to be an act of sabotaging.

(a)   The apathy on the part of the State Govt. is also evident from the findings of the working group on State Resources constituted by the Planning Commission "the suggestion of first generation SFCS (State Finance Corporation) if fully implemented will go a long way in improving the revenue generation capacity of local bodies. However the S.F.S.C. have failed to take a comprehensive view of the resources sharing between the State and Local Bodies or to link them with the functional responsibilities of these bodies. The fiscal domain of the local bodies still remain limited and unsettled. The State Govts. have been slow and hesitant in accepting the recommendation of the S.F.C.S."

(b)   In Bihar, PRIS do not have any choice in regard to the appointment or posting of officers to be associated with the system. It is once again the State Govt. which controls these functionaries like any other functionary under its domain. Through such mane maneuvering Panchayat's autonomy is being gradually curtailed. This frustrates the concept of debureaucratisation, a theme most nurtured by protagonists of democratic decentralisation. The present scenario confirms the belief that provisions made in the Bihar Panchayat Raj, 1993 do not have the chance to be given effect to. We have hardly come through any genuine concern on the part of the State Powers for empowering Panchayats to the minimum of the provisions in the Act. Rather, every cautious step appears to have been taken to frustrate the ground for autonomy to them. The continuing dominance of the officers and officials attached with the system has not allowed them to grow on their own talents leading them to remain dwarf. Every experiment at strengthening the system has so far been forestalled under designs and if things are not allowed to improve, it is doubtful the system could really ever grow.

(c) No clear cut trend has so far been allowed to emerge as to the status and functions of PRIS. On the other hand, the constitution has always visualization PRIS as the institution of Self Govt. (Articles 243 d and 243 G). However, such an ambiguous situation has landed Panchayats in a State from where it could not assert its position as an institution of Self Govt. (ISG). Panchayats, as Institution of Self Govt., means they should enjoy functional, financial and administrative autonomy in their working which is far from their to imagination in the given situation. Thanks to the hostile attitude of the State power which as it appear by nature and belief does not approve the concept of decentralisation.

For knowing the actual constraints being faced in the working of Panchayats we had a few questions for our respondents. We put our questions in Hindi medium to have convenient interaction on issues having been emerged.

 & vki gky ds vuqHkoksa ls crk;sa fd vkt ds iapk;r dh fLFkfr Lok;Ùkrk ds ifjis{k esa iwoZ ds iapk;r ls fHkUu fn[krk gS\ gka@ughaA

 & ;fn gka] rks fdl :i esa

 & ;fn ugha] rks fdl Lrj ls O;o/kku ns[kus dks feyrh gS\

  ljdkjh gLr{ksi

  vf/kdkfj;ksa dk euekusiu

  foÙkh; ladV

  xzke lHkk dh vksj ls vM+pu

  vU;A

Sensing not a definite reply against the question we had another one to ascertain the extent of empowerment of Panchayats :

 & fcgkj iapk;r jkt vf/kfu;e 1993 ds dafMdk 21 esa of.kZr iapk;r ds dk;ksZ dk ,d yEch lwph is'k gSA buesa ls ,slk dkSu dk;Z gS& ftls vki vko';drkuqlkj fcuk fdlh ckgjh gLr{ksi ls vius Lrj ls djkus esa Lora= gSa\

None of the respondents we used out of our sample could respond what was actually desired from them. Instead, those few who responded at all juxtaposed the level of performance between the previous and the present set ups. However, incidentally, they understood the spirit of the alternative question in regard to the level of autonomy granted to Panchayat as an institution in matters of discharging its responsibilities independently. Out of the total 97 respondents constituting our sample unit 16 (15.52 percent) particularly Mukhias, Up-Mukhias vaguely meant the state of autonomy availed by Panchayat in matter of discharging some of its functions within the list of functions under the Act. As against this 30 (29.10) of them replied in negative- a blank 'No' while 51 (49.47) respondents did not know about the provision in the Act granting a long list of functions to a Panchayat. The saddest part which is baffling is the unawareness of the majority of members about the actual status of Panchayat under the law of the land. Unawareness brings passivity among the members when reshaping of the institution has come as a challenge for them.

The emerging micro-level data does suggest that Panchayat is far from being an autonomous institution entitled for discharging its functions under the Law of the Land. This is so even after the adverse comments of the Patna High Court.

The Patna High Court, hearing the writ petition filed on behalf of the Bihar State Panchayat Parishad, had charged the State Govt. of Bihar as anti Panchayat anti democracy and also anti-constitution. The then Chief Justice of the Patna High Court along with another judge, Justice R.N. Prasad had mentioned in their judgement that these institutions responsible for village administration have not been conferred upon the proclaimed rights and those rights remain on paper and appears to be verbal."

Apart from the Governmental neglect to the PRIS, it is ill luck on the part of the system that it has never had the leadership with element of activism. They (Leaders) saw for themselves jumping pad like prospect to rise up to the higher level of leadership. With this personal ambition behind they, as they are with hardly any botheration used to, go on with things as they are. Besides, the leadership does not have the skill or third sense to articulate and rationalize situation around them. This is much manifested at their response level also which we have discussed in previous paragraphs. What we have understood about them is that they never take things with the sense of responsibility. Their interests are limited to their personal prosperity and utterly lack the spirit of serving humanity they have been called upon to serve. They spend much of their time in the pursuit of power politics and have little time either for the institution or for the section of population who were to be served.[6] The observation of Iqbal Narain is worth mentioning here : "The system of democratic decentralisation has, in fact, deepened economic disparities by its inability to check the flow of developmental benefits to those who are socially, economically and politically dominant (CAS quoted in Aurora,1974).

NOTES AND REFERENCES

.1.   Dr. Mahipal- "From Raj Governance to Swaraj Governance"- Kurukshetra, August, 2004, pp. 7-8.

2.   Rajesh K. Jha- " Panchayats- Story of Promises and Pitfalls"- Kurukshetra, Jan. 2004, pp. 39-41.

3.   Aureliano Fernandes- "Changing Role of Panchayats in the New Millennium" Kurukshetra, Nov. 2001, p. 15.

4.   Rajesh K. Jha, Op.Cit., pp. 39-41.

5.   Aureliano Fernandes- Op.Cit., p. 16.

6.   G.N. Thakur, Leadership Network: A Study on the Emerging Pattern of Leadership at Panchayat Raj Levelin Bihar, Mimeo- 2003.

CONCLUSION

The wearer knows where the shoe pinches. We have tried to understand problems facing Panchayats through the eyes of its leaders who were elected for the job of managing the affairs of Panchayats after the last Panchayat elections in the State. The socio-economic development of the rural community depends to a great extent as to how the leaders identify problems facing them and also find solutions thereof. Unless leaders play an active role any breakthrough in the system becomes merely a mirage Panchayati Raj leadership, aiming at development of the community, naturally becomes he 'gap-closer' between bureaucrats and the masses thus bridging up a wide organisational gap. It is expected to instill in the people a sense of partnership in developmental activities by seeking their cooperation and support. The leadership is also deemed to play educative role by widening the range and deepening the reach of participatory processes. Besides, by effective planning and honest execution it can utilize the available local resources by taking into consideration the local needs and interests. The leadership can communicate the requirements of the people by voicing their concern at higher rungs of administration. This sort of communication and interaction would positively facilitate in reinforcing administrative accountability and responsiveness in the sphere of socio-economic development.

All these qualities in leadership particularly at Panchayat level is never presumptions but is essentially required for holding the office. We, on our part, have devoted a chapter discussing personal qualities of the leadership that has emerged. Leaders have to discharge the institutional responsibilities Panchayats have been called upon to do after the 73rd Constitutional Amendment Act. It is relevant to distinguish Panchayats then and now which in itself should speak the volume of new responsibilities the present generation of leadership has been called upon to shoulder. Needless to state here that with the real power now going to Panchayats, the leadership is expected to ensure that power vested in the institution are effectively utilised. They should be vibrant institutions performing necessary developmental, regulatory and general administrative functions. Specific responsibilities have also been entrusted to them to prepare plans for economic development and social justice in respect of matters listed in XI Schedule of the constitution where in Panchayats have been called upon to shoulder the responsibilities of 29 departments concerning the welfare of the people living in the areas.

With such a huge responsibilities for Panchayat's leadership it is the acid test which they have to qualify by sheer involvement and with a sense of commitment. There naturally arises a point at issue : who are the present leaders and from what back ground? Due to its socio-cultural foundations the emergent Pancyaiyat Raj leadership will have to undergo a process of

"Resocialization" before it can readily be counted upon to carry forward the "nation-building" activities of economic mobilization and socio-political reorganisation.

We have discussed some of the emerging trends of leadership at Panchayat level in a separate chapter, however it will be worth while to state here that the weaker population, notwithstanding, its numerical strength rarely succeeded in occupying elective positions at Panchayat's level. Never did an exploiting class voluntarily renounce its powers and its capacity to foster their own interests. This way Panchayat system in its previous avtar helped powerful rural classes and linked them to the ruling class of India. The old zamindars saw in the statutory Panchayat system a prospect of compensation for the zamindari they had lost. The outcome of the last Panchayat elections in Bihar has, however, turned the table turtle. Now those zamindars also belonging mostly to castes now falling under general category have had to be contented with merely 1752 percent seats in Naugachia sub-division forming the universe of our study while OBCs. are massively there in position of power, they being 68.04 percent of the total population. It is not that their massive strength at Panchayat is only due to reservation provision for them- they have occupied seats also by utilizing number cards. Those in general category have now to be reconciled in view of their shrinking numerical strength vis-a-vis the OBCs.

Scheduled Castes are also there into the scene but they are mostly there by way of reservation of seats for them and not in their own right.

The present set up of leadership is naturally expected to serve the interests of the preponderant weaker people more than what was done for them by the previous regime. Active as well as mature sections of the population have come to lead and take initiative keeping in mind the wrongs done to them in the past. A good number of leaders are educated and if they put their heart and soul together they could reach the point of success. They have the potentiality to stop all the monkey-business that went unhindered in the past through Panchayat. They could instill in the people a sense of partnership in development programmes and seek their cooperation and support in their implementation. Through effective planning and implementation the present set up of leadership can very much help mobilise local resources in the delivery of inputs and services.

Other point that needs to be discussed here is the attitude of the State Govt. towards strengthening the hands of the emerging leadership we have already discussed about.

What has been the attitude of the State Govt. in regard to the transfer of powers to Panchayats?

As stated in earlier chapter, Panchayats have been given the functions of 29 departments under the Bihar Panchayati Raj Act, 1993. The Govt. on its part, has also issued directions to most of the departments to transfer all these responsibilities to Panchayats through respective departments. If taken together, 21 departments of the State Govt. have so far issued directions to the district collectors and other sub-ordinate officers to give effect to the transfer of responsibilities to P.R.I.S. including Panchayats.

But the fact of the matter is that the Govt. decisions to transfer powers to Panchayats remaining on paper only. It is all paper transaction. The reality of the situation is that Panchayats still suffer from 'Dependency Syndrome'. They are still far away from taking over the responsibilities of those areas of functions mentioned in the Bihar Act itself. For the State Govt., apparently, there hardly has any substance in the constitutional mandate through the 73rd Amendment of the constitution envisaging empowerment of Panchayats with financial and administrative responsibilities for the sake of good governance.

The question that comes to ones mind is that why does the Govt. adopt a contradictory stand particularly when transfer of power comes up for implementation.

The ready answer is- the British legacy of distrust by the people placed higher in status and rank of those placed below in the hierarchy still persists. The distrust has enmeshed grass-roots democratic structures as well. This has in turn resulted in indifferent and fragmented functioning among Panchayat and village level workers. Cordial relationship between people's representatives and officers/officials was considered to be a pre-requisite for the success of the system. However, the leadership appears to be obsessed of their non-cooperative behaviour. They do not observe transparency in most of the matters including availability of funds and resources. The Govt. field functionaries responsible for delivery of services at village Panchayat   level work in a disparate and segmented manner with a narrow departmental approach. Each worker looks at problems and implements the assigned scheme in a compartmentalized manner as their sectors in hierarchy never take a holistic and integrated view. With such a non-cooperative attitude on their part leaders can't move forward to formulate plans and policies according to the felt needs. Apart from these local factors the hostile attitude of the State Govt. against Panchayat is at the root of destabilizing the system of Panchayati Raj.

The Patna High Court hearing the writ petition field on behalf of the Bihar Panchayat Parishad had also charged the State Govt. of Bihar as anti-Panchayat, anti-democracy and also anti-constitution. The then Chief Justice of the Patna High Court along with another judge, Justice R.V Prasad had mentioned in their judgement that these institutions responsible for village administration have not been conferred upon the proclaimed rights and those rights remain on paper and appears to be verbal."

If we share our experiences of State Govt. interferences in the working of P.R.I.S. right after the 1961 Act including the present one there is a common case that governmental restrictions imposed on these institutions hardly paved way for decentralisation. The hope for a village Panchayat to assume the role of a democratic institution, as has also been envisaged under the

1993 Constitutional Amendment Act, to be concerned with economic development and social change, is not likely to be fulfilled so soon. The Govt. has every time failed to realise the very perspectives of exercising control as instead of assuming the role of helper, friend and guide the Govt. looked at them as its agents.

State laws enacted from time to time hardly had the scope for determination of the will of the people. For any small action Panchayat has to necessarily obtain the approval of the concerning authority at the State headquarters. This amply manifests that element of distrust determines the relationship between the State Govt. and the Panchayati Raj bodies. The tendency on the part of the State Govt. has been to retain maximum possible control over local Govt. institutions. More so, financial powers exercised by the Govt. over the local bodies becomes formidable enough to browbeat the latter into any submissive action.

In the matter of fund also Panchayats and other higher units in the system have come to rely solely on the grants from the Govt. both State and union. In such a situation the grant getting agency has naturally to act as agencies to grants sanctioning authorities. Acting as the agency of the Govt. P.R.I.S. have to fulfill series of official obligations in the matter of expenditure. The Grant giving authorities acquire the right to issue directions from time to time during execution of the respective schemes. Such a subjugation results in progressive loss of interest in planning and development expected from Panchayats. The idea behind establishment of State Finance Commission for distributing proceeds of taxes, duties, tolls and fees levied by the State Govt. between the Govt. and the P.R.I.S. still remains non-functional.

Leadership at these levels have hardly the scope and opportunity to take initiative and be imaginative. At best they have to remain engaged in petty administrative matters. Panchayat as of now, seems to be decentralised administration through centralised directives. Instead of becoming Govt. at their own level as envisaged at every new opportunity, P.R.I.S. are forced to work as the limbs of Govt. The two great enemies of realistic planning for development- order coming from head quarters and imposed assignments without taking into consideration local conditions are still dominating the scene. Programmes for P.R.I.S. are drawn up and targets fixed by the Govt. itself. The gulf between paper achievements and actualities is still widen. They are yet to get the opportunity to act up to themselves. Such a growing trend has terribly upset the very spirit behind the 73rd constitutional amendment which sought to bring both democracy and devolution of powers to Panchayat. Panchayat has been given the status of an institution of self Govt. Institutional status gives institutional existence i.e. the decisions have to be taken by the people's representatives, (b) Institutional capacity i.e. the institution is empowered to make rules independently and, (c) Financial viability i.e. it is sufficiently empowered to raise financial resources to meet its responsibilities. In other words, Panchayat as institution of self Govt. means they should enjoy functional, financial and administrative autonomy in their working. But the Govt. by design, chose to keep the Panchayat in perpetual chaos like situation and also succeeds in weakening them by utilizing administrative apparatus under its control with the result that Panchayat could not become assertive in its demand for institutional status which guarantees autonomy in the areas of Funds, Functioning and functionaries- the 3 F.S.

The initial euphoria among the newly elected leadership for combating with the Govt. in the process of securing rightful place for Panchayat was once manifested in their decision to organize Mukhia Sangh at every block level as a pressure group. But no sooner the Sangh came with a bang it also disappeared with a whimper for the reasons not yet clear.

Apart from the hostility from governmental sources, it is ill luck for the P.R.I.S. that they have never had leadership with element of activism.. The leaders saw in it jumping pad like prospects to rise to the higher level of leadership rank. With this personal ambition behind, they as they are used to, keep things just moving with less of enthusiasm and without the sincerity it deserved. They also suffer from inherent weaknesses also. They do not have the skill for overcoming the odds coming in the way. They do not have a required level of awareness about things around them. We have also gone through their level of response to querries related to the working of Panchayat. It appeared to us that they hardly take things with a sense of responsibility. Their interest lies else where also. Their personal prosperity is their basic concern while claiming to lead people at Panchayat level. They utterly lack the spirit of serving the cause of the institution which has ultimately to be instrument of economic growth and social justice. It is not only the spirit that they lack they also lack the ability to cope with the challenges. They hardly have the patience to cultivate the art of leadership and the nature of responsibilities thrushed upon them as public representatives. Though they are fairly educated but do not have the motivation to prepare themselves for the task. Most of them were found inert. They need adequate training before they pick up their jobs. Leadership is more for personalizaling of the affairs than to treat things public. They have more to pursue power politics. In the process fairness tin their dealings is very much questionable. As a consequence of these defects leadership is equally responsible for the drooping of Panchayat system to the extent so that Panchayats are not given the status of being pillar of Grass-roots democracy. They do not have any thing of their own except the behind them. Neither they have cultivated the image-consciousness nor have they cared to cope with their in any positive sense. They do not have the resource base to be genuinely concerned for the welbing of their constituents. They remain contented to serve as the conduit of the State Govt. and have learnt to survive by merely implementing schemes handed over to them by the State and the Centre Govts. Panchayats have not only gradually lost the element of self confidence but also facing crisis of dignity. Panchayat leadership either in the past or at present do not have had such mind-set to fight for restoration of appropriate status it deserves both under the law of the land and also in view of its antecedents. For the people at large, Panchayat's efficiency is hardly their concern. Indian people in general and those of Bihar in particular do not have personal understanding with institutional system of governance. They are least bothered weather an institution functions or not. So is their antipathy both against governance or non-governance, democracy or no democracy. All these are yet to become matters of general public concern. This is the most unfortunate part of our system of governance which generally operates without people's participation. With such indifferent population leaders are at their liberty to take things as it suits them. These inherent weaknesses Panchayats suffer from go to the advantages of the State Govt. who makes all pretensions to undermine the significance of Panchayati Raj system. Needless to add here that State Powers have the only strategy towards Panchayati Raj and that is to keep it in a state of confusion and uncertainty. Besides, for governing Panchayat system it is only the State Power entitled to chart out its course of destiny as it falls within the State subject. The Union Govt., at best, would lay down national policy which has always been in favour of Panchayati Raj system. Even in the 73rd Amendment Act, the use of 'may' is very significant in this Articles 243 G. and 243 H. provide autonomies to Panchayati Raj bodies in various ways but the extent and scope of the autonomies are left to the discretion of states regard. And over all track record of states has been very dismal in fulfilling spirit and expectations of 73rd Amendment. That is why the National Commission to Review the working of the constitution suggested to make the provision mandatory for the states by recommending this new version of the Article 243 G.- "Subject to the provision of the constitution the legislature of the State shall, by law, vest the Panchayats with such powers and authority as are necessary to enable them to function as institutions of Self Govt. and such law shall contain provisions for the devolution of powers and responsibilities upon Panchayats at the appropriate level subject to such conditions as shall be specified there in, with   respect to :

a)   Preparation of Plans for economic development and social justice;

b)   The implementation of schemes for economic development and social justice as shall be entrusted to them including those in relation to the matters listed in the XIth schedule."

What is remarkable in these lines is that the word 'May' is felt to be purposeless. 'May' always gives liberty to the State Govt. to act as it suits its design. Therefore replacement of the term 'May' by 'Shall" is so much favoured to prevent the State Govt. from acting against the welbing of Panchayati Raj system.

Though article 243 G. of the constitution provides an opportunity to Panchayats to prepare plans for economic development of rural areas in order to formulate and execute plans Panchayats do not have adequate functions, finance and functionaries at their disposal. The State Govts. have not made efforts towards making them autonomous in that areas of operation; thus Panchayats, instead of becoming local self Govts. became instruments in the hands of the State Govts. The Report of the Task Force on Devolution of Powers and functions upon P.R.I.S. brought out by the Ministry of Rural Development admitted that "the mandatory provisions of the 73rd Amendment Act are yet to be implemented in letter and spirit by most of the states after the said Act was brought into force in April, 1993.

In view of these states facts there is no bias in commenting that Panchayats are sulking between the hostile State Govt. and weak-kneed leadership. The situation, particularly in Bihar context, has reached such a dismal point that Panchayat meetings are not held properly. When convened it is mostly dissolved for want of quorum. From this it will be evident that Panchayat has been losing its potentiality not only for the people but also for its rank and file who hardly see things with any amount of optimism.

BIBLIOGRAPHY

A.P. Barubas : Panchayati Raj at a Glance (Working paper),1962, The Indian School of Public Administration.

Adiseshiah, Inolcolms : "Realising Goals of 73rd Amendment Thought Literacy", Kurukshetra, June, 1994.

A.A. Sethi J.D. : Gandhi Today Vikas Publishing Housing, New Delhi.

Bhatnagar, S. : Rural Local Government in India, Life and Light Publishers, New Delhi, 1978.

Bhargava, B.S. : Politico-Administrative Dynamics in Panchayati Raj, Ashish Publishing House, New Delhi, 1978.

Bhargava, B.S. : Panchayati Raj Institution : An Analysis of Issues, Problem and Recommendation of Ashok Mehta Committee, Ashish Publishing House, New Delhi, 1979.

BIBLIOGRAPHY

Bhargava, B.S. : Grass Roots Leadership : A Study of Leadership in Panchayati Raj Institutions, Ashish Publishing House, New Delhi, 1978.

Bhargava, B.S. : Panchayati Raj System and Political Parties, Ashok Publishing House, New Delhi, 1979.

Barowalia, J.N. : Commentary on Himachal Pradesh Panchayati Raj Act, 1968 (Act) of 1970, Minerva Book House, Shimla, 1988.

Bhatnagar, S. : Panchayati Raj in Kangra District, Orient Longman, New Delhi, 1974.

Bhargava, B.S. and Rao, S. Rama : India Local Government of Study, Minerva Associated (Publication), Pvt. Ltd., Calcutta, 1978.

B. Mukherjee : Community Development in India, 1961, Orient Longman.

B. Maheshwari : Studies in Panchayati Raj, 1963, Metropolitan Book Co.

Bhattacharya Mohit and Dutta Prabha, K. : Governing Rural India, Uppal Publishing House, New Deoh, 1991.

BIBLIOGRAPHY

Bhargava, B.S. and Subha : Women in Panchayati Raj : Some Reflection on Karnataka experience, Kurukshetra, June, 1994.

Bhatt, K.S., : Panchayati Raj Administration in Maharashtra, Popular Prakashan, Bombay, 1974.

Bhattacharya, Mohit : Rural Self Government in Metropolitan, Calcutta Asian Publishing House, New Yark, 1965.

Bose, Ajit : Paschim Bangal Panchayat, Byabastha, (In Bengali) Pashim Bangal Rajya Pustak Parishad, Calcutta, 1985.

Carl C. Taylor Douglas Esminger : India's Roots of Democracy, (Ed), 1968, Orient Longmans

David C. Potter : Government in Rural India, 1964, The London School of Economics and Political Sciences.

Dasgupta, Ashim : Rural Development Planning under Left Front Government in West Bengal Govt. of W.B. 1981.

BIBLIOGRAPHY

Darshankar, Arjun : Leadership in Panchayati Raj : A Study of Bed District of Maharashtra, Panchsheel Prakashan, Jaipur, 1979.

Desai, A.R. : Rural Sociology in India, Popular Prakashan, Bombay, 1969.

Dube, S.N. and Ratna Mudia : Structure and Process of Decision Making in Panchayati Raj Institutions, Somaiya Publication, Bombay, 1976.

Dey, K.K. : Panchayati Raj, Asian Publishing House, Bombay, 1961.

Dayal, R. : Panchayati Raj in India, Metropolitan Book Co. Pvt. Ltd., Delhi,1970.

Dutta, Abhijit : Decentralisation and Local Government Reform in India, Journal of Public Administration, Vol. XXXI, No. 25, July-Sept. 1985.

Democratic World, New Delhi, January, 22, 1978.

BIBLIOGRAPHY

G.N. Thakur : "Panchayati Raj : Hopes and Despair in Rural Development in India, Problems and Prspects (Ed), 1995, Annual Publications.

G. Gandhi, M.K. : Panchayati Raj, Navjivan Publishing House, Ahmedabad, 1956 (Compiled by R.K. Prabhu).

Gurumurthy, V. : Panchayati Raj and The Weaker Section, Ashish Publication House, New Delhi,1987.

Ganguly, B. and Ganguly, M. : Voting Behaviour in a Developing Society, Sterling Publishers, New Delhi, 1975.

Hugh Tinker : Foundation of Local Self Govt. in India, Pakistan and Burma, 1967, Lalvani Publishing House.

Harold Zink : Rural Local Govt. in Sweden, Italy and India, 1957, London Stevens & Sons.

Henry Maddick : Democracy, Decentralization and Development, 1968, Asia Publishing House.

BIBLIOGRAPHY

Henry Meddick	:	Panchayati Raj : A Study of Rural Local Movement in India, Longman, London, 1970.
Iqbal Narain, Shushil Kumar, P.C. Mathur	:	Panchayati Raj Administration (Ed) 1970, The Indian Institute of Public Administration.
Imandar, N.R., Cedl Inmdar, N.R. (Ed)	:	Function of Village Panchayats, Popular Prakashan, New Delhi, 1970.
Jain, L.C.	:	Panchayat's Women Will Win, Kurukshetra, June, 1994.
J.N. Drummond	:	The Finance of Local Govt., 1964, George Allen and Unwin Ltd.
John Matthai	:	Village Govt. in British India, 1915, London.
Jather, R.V.	:	Village Govt. in British India, 1915, London.
Jather, R.V.	:	Evolution of Panchayati Raj in India, J.S.S. Institute of Economic Research, Dharwar, 1964.
Jain, S.P.	:	Panchayati Raj in Assam, National Institute of Community Development, Hydrabad, 1976.

Khanna, R.L.	:	Panchayati Raj in Punjab and Haryana, Mahendra Capital Publishers, Sector 11-D, Chandigarh, 1966.
Khanna R.D.	:	Panchayati Raj in India, The English Book Shop, Chandigarh, 1956.
Khanna, R.L.	:	Panchayati Raj in India, The English Book Depot, Ambala Centt, 1972.
Kashyap, Anirban	:	Panchayati Raj View of Founding Father and Recommendations of Different Committee, Lancers Books, New Delhi, 1989.
Kumar, Vijay	:	Scheduled Castes Panchayati Pradhans in India, Ajanta Publishing (India), 1989.
Kumar, Kirti	:	Strategies for Empowerment of Women in Panchayati Raj Institution, Kurukshetra, June, 1994.
Khilberg, Mats	:	The Panchayati Raj in India : debate in a Developing Society, Young Asia Publication, New Delhi, 1970.
Kautilya	:	Artha Sastra, Samaskrita Pustak Bhandar, Calcutta, 1965.

BIBLIOGRAPHY

Kolhi, Atul : Panchayats in West Bengal Development and Planning, Department of West Bengal, 1991.

M.V. Mathur & Iqbal Narain : Panachayati Raj, Planning & Democracy (Ed), 1969, Asia Publishing House.

Mukhopadhyay, Ashok : The Panchayat Administration in West Bengal, The World Press, Pvt. Ltd., Calcutta, 1991.

Malviya, H.D. : Village Panchayats in India All India Congress Committee, New Delhi, 1956.

Mathur, M.V. & Iqbal Narain : Panchayati Raj Planning Democracy, Asia Publishing House, London, 1969.

Mishra, S.H. : New Horizons in Rural Development Administration, Mittal Publication, New Delhi, 1989.

Mathur, M.V. & Iqbal Narain & Sinha, V.M. : Panchayati Raj in Rajasthan : A Study in Jaipur District, Impax India, New Delhi, 1966.

Mukherjee, Neela	:	Rural Women and Panchayati Raj Institution, Kurukshetra, June, 1994.
Mathew, George	:	Women in Panchayati Raj Beginning of a Silent Revolution, Kurukshetra, June, 1994.
Mahipal	:	Empowerment Women Through Panchayati Raj Institution, Kurukshetra, June, 1994.
Moorthy, O.K.	:	Some Observation on the Effect Panchayati Raj on Weaker Section in Local Government Institutions in Rural India, edited at Haldipur R.N. and Paramassharmro, V.R.K. National Institute of Community Development, Hydrabad, 1970.
Millbrath I.L.W. & M.I. Goel	:	Political Participation, How and What do people get involved in Politics, R. & Mc. Hally, 2nd Ed. Chicago, 1977.
Narayana, Revathi	:	Women in Panchayati Raj : The Divide Between Intent and Implementation, Kurukshetra, June, 1994.

BIBLIOGRAPHY

N.R. Inamdar	:	Functioning of Village Panchayats, 1970, Bombay Popular Prakashan.
Radha Kumud Mukherjee	:	Local Govt. in Ancient India, 1920, Motilal Banarsi Das.
Raghuvir Sahai	:	Panchayati Raj in India, 1968, Kitab Mahal.

Report of the Decentralization Commission upon India, 1909, Para 649.

Report of the Team for the study of Community Projects and National Extension Service, Vol. 1, Government of India, New Delhi.

Report of the Committee on Panchayati Raj Institutions, Government of India, New Delhi, 1978.

Report of the Committee to Review the Existing Administration Arrangements for Rural Development and Poverty Alleviation Programmes (GAARD), Government of India, New Delhi, 197.5.

Rao, D.V.R. :   Panchayats and Rural Development, Ashish Publishing House, New Delhi, 1980.

Report of the Committee on Panchayat Raj Institution, Government of India, New Delhi, 1978.

Report of the Committee on Panchayat Raj Institution, Government of India, Ministry of Agriculture and Irrigation, Department of Rural Development, August, 1978, New Delhi, p. 4.

Rachana, Suchinmayee : Reservation as a Strategy for Political Empowerment the ongoing Debate, in Niraj Saha, (Ed) The Women in India Politics (Empowerment of Through Political Participation) Gyan Publishing House, New Delhi, 2000.

Panchayati Raj Power of People Ministry of Rural Development, Government of India, The Hindustan Times, October 8, 1994.

P.R. Dubhashi	:	Rural Development Administration in India, 1970, Bombay Popular Prakashan.
Prasad, R.C.	:	Democracy and Development : The Grass Roots Experience in India, Rachana Prakashan, New Delhi, 1971.
Pant, Niranjan	:	The Politics of Panchayati Raj Administration : A Study of Officials and Non-Officials Relugation, Concept Publishing Company, Delhi, 1979.
Prasad, Sivahugo	:	Panchayats and Development, Life and Light Publishers, New Delhi, 1980.

BIBLIOGRAPHY

Parvathamma	:	Panchayati Raj and Weaker Section, Presented at the Seminar held in NIRD. Hyderabad, 1975 (Unpublished Paper).
Prasad, Kanta	:	Women and Panchayats Making Success of the New Experiment, Kurukshetra, June, 1994.
Palanithural, P.	:	Empowerment of Women : A Novel Exercise, Kurukshethra, Jun, 1994.
Pramanik, Swapan	:	Panchayat and People : The West Bengal Experience, P.M. Bagehi & Co. Pvt. Ltd., 1994.
		Quoted in the Report of Committee to Review the Existing Administration Arrangements for Rural Development and Poverty Alleviation Programmes, (CAARD), Department of Rural Development, Ministry of Agriculture, Dec. 1985.
S.K. Dey	:	Community Development, 1964, Asia Publishing House.
S. Kesva Iyenger	:	Fifteen Years of Democratic Planning 1965, Vol. 2. Asia Publishing House.

S.K. Dey	:	Panchayati Raj, 1961, Asia Publishing House.
S.C. Prasad	:	Democracy and Development, 1967, Radha Prakashan
Srinivas, M.N.	:	Social Change in Modern India, Orient Longman, New Delhi, 1977.
Shriram Maheshwar	:	Local Government in India, The Macmillan Co. of India Ltd., Delhi, 1971.
Sushil Kumar & Venkatarman, K.	:	State Panchayati Raj Relation : A Study of Supervision and Control in Tamil Nadu, Asia Publishing House, Bombay, 1974.
Seshadri, K.	:	Political Linkages and Rural Development : A Comparative Study of the Political Process and Interaction Between different levels of Govt. in two India (Andhra and Gujarat), States, National Publishing House, New Delhi, 1976.

Sammiuddin, Abida : A Critique of Panchayati Raj with Special Reference to Uttar Pradesh, Sahitya Bhawan, Agra, 1976.

Sharma, Surjit Singh : Rural Elites in India, Sterling Publishers Pvt. Ltd. New Delhi, 1979.

Sharma Ravindra : Village Panchayats in Rajasthan, Alesh Publishers, Jaipur,1984.

Shukla, L.P. : A History of Village Panchayats in India, Institute of Economic Research, Dharwar, 1964.

Shiviah, M. Rao, K.V. Narayana, Murty L.S. Nand, G. Murti Kajunigh : Panchayati Raj An Analytical Survey, National Institute of Community Development, Hyderabad,1976.

Sivang, N. : Panchayati Raj Reforms and Rural Development, Chagh Publishing, Allahabad, 1990.

Sectharam, M. : Role of Women in Panchayati Raj Institution, Kuruksheta, June,1994.

Sancheti, D.C. : The Weaker Section of the Community and Panchayati Raj in Rajasthan, in Panchayati Raj Planning and Democracy, Cited by Mathur M.V. & Narayan Iqbal, Asia Publishing House, Bombay, 1969.

Tak, B.L. : Sociological Dimensions of Gram Raj, Vimal Prakashan Ghaziabad, 1979.

U.K. Hicks : Development from Below, 1961, Oxford University Press.

V.T. Krishnamchari : Community Development in India, 1958, The Publication Division.

V.K. Gaikwad : Panchayati Raj and Bureaucracy, 1969, National Institute of Community Development, Hyderabad.

Verma, B.M. : Decentralization in Administration, (IIPA), Uppal Publishing House, New Delhi, 1990.

Mimeo :

G.N. Thakur, : Unpublished Thesis on "Working of Zila Parishads and Panchayat Samitis in Bihar"- 1975.

Journals :

Aiyer, I	:	Democratic Decentralisation Experiment in India, Economic Weekly, June 14, 1961.
Balwant Ray Mehta Committee	:	Committee on Plan Project Government of Indian, 1957.
K.K. Sinha	:	Evolution of Panchayati Raj in Bihar" in Kurukshetra, September, 2001.
Kaushik Asha	:	Legislative Elite and Social Change : A Study of Woman Legislature in the Rajasthan Assembly "Journal of Constitutional and Parliamentary Studies, Vol. XVI, No. 1, 2.
Rajesh K. Jha	:	Panchayats- Stories of Promises and Pitfalls" in Kurukshetra, January, 2004.
Mahipal	:	Role of Panchayats in Rural Reconstruction" in Yojna, January, 2002.
Mahanty, Bidyat	:	Panchayati Raj-72 Constitutional Amendments and Women, EPM. 30, December, 1995.

Mishra, Surya

: Rural Development : West Bengal Experience, Main Stream, Oct. 31, 1992.

R.M. Verma

: "Panchayati Raj : Rhetoric and Reality" In Kurukshetra, August, 2004.

Rajya Panchayat Training Institute:

: UNNAYAN ONAR (IN BENGAL) Collection of Papers submitted to a Seminar on the 25-28 June,1992, Panchayat Decl. Govt. West Bengal, Kalyani, Nadia, Oct. 1992.

Mahipal

: Panchayati Raj and Development" in Kurukshetra, August, 2004.

डॉ० एच.एस. महला

: राजस्थान में लोकतांत्रिक विकेन्द्रीकरण : नए आयाम एवं नवाचार (प्रतियोगिता दर्पण), अप्रील, 2000/1578

डॉ० अरूण राघव

: लोकनायक जयप्रकाश समाजवादी विचार लोकतांत्रिक संबंधी विचार (प्रतियोगिता दर्पण), अक्टूबर, 1992/336

विनोद सुरोलिया

: राजस्थान में पंचायती राज, (प्रतियोगिता दर्पण), अगस्त,

1994/67

राजीव रंजन	:	पंचायत चुनाव बिहार : सरस सलील, मार्च (द्वितीय) 2001
डॉ० नन्द लाल	:	लोकतंत्र के विषय में, गाँधी नेहरू और टैगोर का चिन्ता, (प्रतियोगिता दर्पण), अक्टूबर/ 1995/ 408
कृष्ण किशोर पाण्डेय, स० सम्पादक, दैनिक हिन्दुस्तान	:	गाँधी जी और पंचायती राज की अवधारणा (योजना), अक्टूबर, 1995
राजीव कुमार चतुर्वेदी	:	पंचायत संचार सेवा केन्द्र, योजना, अक्टूबर, 1995
डॉ० मनमोहन सिंह, पूर्व केन्द्रीय वित्त मंत्री, वर्त्तमान प्रधान मंत्री (भारत सरकार)	:	विकास : एक मानवीय दृष्टिकोण, योजना, अक्टूबर, 1995
बालकृष्ण कुवावटः	:	गाँधी जी का ग्राम स्वराज (स्वप्न एवं यथार्थ), योजना, अक्टूबर, 1995
डॉ० ममोहन चन्द पाण्डे	:	गाँधीवादी चिन्तन और औद्योगिक विकास योजना, अक्टूबर, 1995
डॉ० उमेश चन्द अग्रवाल	:	ग्रामीण विकास लेख, ग्रामीण विकास हेतु परिचालित विभिन्न योजना (प्रतियोगिता दर्पण), फरवरी/ 2000/ 1197

डॉ० रामरतन शर्मा, रीडर, अर्थशास्त्र अध्ययनशाला	:	गाँधी जी का आर्थिक चिन्तन एवं इनकी प्रासंगिकता, योजना, अक्टूबर, 1995
प्रो० उमरावमल शाह	:	ग्राम विकास की सहकारिता की भूमिका, योजना, अक्टूबर, 1995

NEWS PAPERS :

The Hindu- May 07, 2005

The Hindustan Times- Dated 17.6.2001

Also consulted other papers of different States :

1. The Hindustan Times (Patna) from period 2001-2005.

2. The Times of India (Patna) from 2001-2005.

3. Hindustan (Patna and Bhagalpur).

4. Dainik Jagaran (Patna and Bhagalpur).

5. See Specially Dainik Jagaran - 31.8.2004 to 19.9.2004.